The Gambardier

6-INCH HOWITZER POSITION NEAR MAMETZ, 1916

The Gambardier

'Mark Severn'
(Major Franklin Lushington)

LEONAUR

The Gambardier
by Mark Severn (Major Franklin Lushington)

Published by Leonaur Ltd in 2007

ISBN: 978-1-84677-221-4 (hardcover)
ISBN: 978-1-84677-222-1 (softcover)

http://www.leonaur.com

Publisher's Notes

In the interests of authenticity, the spellings, grammar and place names
used have been retained from the original edition.

The opinions expressed in this book are those of the author
and are not necessarily those of the publisher.

Contents

Prologue

On the eleventh day of the eleventh month of the Eleventh Year since the signing of the Armistice, I have just returned from laying a wreath on the Artillery Memorial at Hyde Park Corner. The inscription on the wreath reads: *In Grateful Memory of All Ranks of the 90th Brigade R. G. A.* It is the annual tribute of the Colonel of the Brigade who lives too far away in the country to allow of him laying it himself.

Standing under the shadow of that great symbolic howitzer I wondered how many of the large crowd, gathered there in reverent silence, had any conception of the work done by the artillery during the war, and how many could picture the life led by the average gunner during those four years. The year has brought forth a spate of war books illustrating the story of the fighting man from nearly every angle. There has also been a wonderful war play. I do not, however, remember any account which deals solely with the war from the gunner point of view, or, at any rate, from the point of view of that large proportion of the artillery who fought and served with the big guns.

In August, 1914, our heavy artillery in France consisted of four batteries, sixteen guns in all. In November, 1918, there "were more than five hundred batteries in this theatre of war alone, numbering two thousand two hundred and fifteen heavy guns and howitzers.

The amount of ammunition shipped to France to supply this vast armament averaged over one million shells a month during the last nine months of the war.

In the Battle of Ypres, 1917, fifty-three thousand tons of metal was fired from the muzzles of these monsters in one week.

The cost of the ammunition fired in one day during the final battles of 1918 was over three million pounds sterling.

The mind very soon ceases to grasp the significance of figures like these. I shall endeavour, in the following pages, to make them more real by giving some account, a lame one I fear, of this great national effort.

Reading through old letters, and talking with old friends, one is carried back down the years. I see, as through the wrong end of a telescope, a tiny but distinct figure which is myself. So strange is this youth in khaki and Sam Browne that I can only write of him in the third person, as of someone whom I once knew well, but who has now passed out of my life. It is my hope that his experiences and adventures will help to give some colour to a story, which is worthy of a more skilled and knowledgeable pen.

If those, whose experience of a heavy howitzer is confined to Mr. Jaggers' representation in bronze and stone, obtain from these pages some picture of a gunner's life in war time, I shall not have written in vain.

If those others, who, like myself, served the big guns during the war years, are hereby reminded of their own story; if they get some reflected glow of those far-off days of high endeavour, forgetting the blood and mud and fear, and remembering only youth and comradeship, and the consciousness of a single purpose, I shall count this reward indeed.

London
November 11th, 1929

Introduction

The main function of artillery in war is the destruction of the enemy personnel. From an artillery point of view the destruction of personnel in the open demands quantity rather than weight of fire-power. previous to November, 1914, the principles of static warfare had always been regarded as subsidiary to those of mobile warfare. Mobility implies reduction of firepower, for it is obvious that the heavier the armament the less mobile the artillery.

Actuated by these considerations, the armies of the Great Powers had concentrated on light guns and howitzers capable of moving with the cavalry and the infantry, and designed for use against the enemy cavalry and infantry in the open. Germany alone, influenced by her pre-conceived strategic plan to burst through the forts guarding the frontiers of Belgium and France, had supplied her artillery with a number of heavy howitzers.

Before describing the composition of the artillery of the British Army in 1914 it would be as well to make clear the difference between the two weapons employed by all artillery, the gun and the howitzer. In a general sense the term gun includes both guns and howitzers, but in a particular sense the gun is a weapon with a long barrel which propels a projectile at great velocity along a fiat trajectory. The howitzer is a weapon with a short, squat barrel which propels a projectile at a low velocity compared to the gun, along a steep trajectory. It will be seen that the howitzer is essentially an offensive arm, for its high trajectory and the consequent steep angle of

GUN PLAN

Showing Ranges from Trafalgar Square of different natures of Ordnance

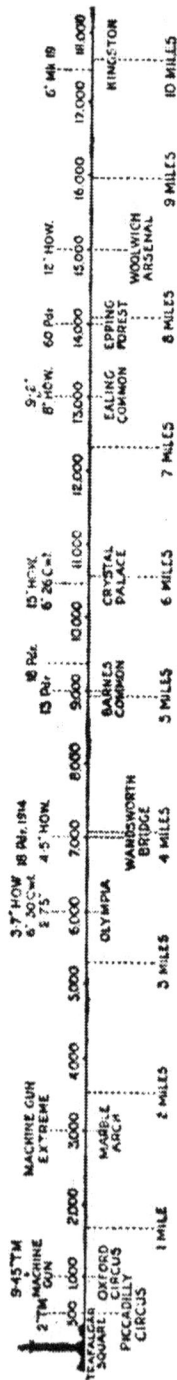

TRAFALGAR SQUARE

9·45"TM
2"TM MACHINE GUN

500 1000 2000 3000 4000 5000 6000 7000 8000 9000 10000 11000 12000 13000 14000 15000 16000 18,000

MACHINE GUN EXTREME

3·7"HOW 18 Pdr.1914
6·30Cwt & 5"HOW.
& 75"

15"HOW.
6"26Cwt.

9·2"
8"HOW.

12"HOW.

6" Mk 19

PICCADILLY CIRCUS OXFORD CIRCUS MARBLE ARCH OLYMPIA WANDSWORTH BRIDGE BARNES COMMON CRYSTAL PALACE EALING COMMON EPPING FOREST WOOLWICH ARSENAL KINGSTON

1 MILE 2 MILES 3 MILES 4 MILES 5 MILES 6 MILES 7 MILES 8 MILES 9 MILES 10 MILES

60 Pdr.

18 Pdr.
13 Pdr.

descent of the shell makes it peculiarly suitable for use against fortifications and trenches. Whereas the gun is more suitable as a defensive arm, its low trajectory and high velocity making it more effective against troops in the open. It is a significant fact that, at the outbreak of war, the German artillery was armed with a preponderance of howitzers, whilst the British and French artillery were armed with a preponderance of guns. In August, 1914, our artillery was divided into two main groups, the Field Artillery manned by the R. H. A. and R. F. A., and the Garrison Artillery consisting of mountain, heavy, siege and coast defence artillery manned by the R. G. A. The titles given to these different branches soon became antiquated, and in some cases misleading, but as they existed until well after the war ended, the intelligent reader must do his best to grasp their separate significations.

13-Pounder: The R. H. A. or Horse Artillery was armed with a light gun, the 13-pounder, and worked almost exclusively with the cavalry, one battery being allotted to each cavalry brigade.

18-Pounder. 4·5 in. Howitzer: The R. F. A manned a slightly heavier gun, the 18-pounder and a light howitzer, the 4.5-in., both firing a light shell a maximum range of 7,000 yards (about 4 miles), their business being the close support of the infantry: three brigades of four gun batteries were allotted to each Division. These were known as Divisional Artillery.

60-Pounder: In addition each Division of the B. E. F. was allotted one heavy battery armed with 60-pounders. At the outbreak of war the 60-pounder was the most nearly perfect gun of its type in use by the belligerents. Firing 60 lb. shrapnel or lyddite shell a maximum range of 10,500 yards (over 6 miles) it was the most powerful weapon in the field capable of being manoeuvred by horse draught. Unfortunately there was only sufficient of these guns available to equip six batteries.

4·7 in.: Until others could be manufactured the heavy artillery was armed with the 4·7 in., a gun which had last seen service in the Boer War. The weight of the shell was 45 lbs. and its maximum range about 9,000 yards (5 miles).

2·75 in.: The mountain artillery was equipped with a small gun, the 2·75 in. firing a 15 lb. shell a range of 6,000 yards (3½ miles). These guns took to pieces and were carried on mule-back.

3·7 in.: Howitzer: Towards the end of the war they were replaced by the 3·7 in. howitzer, which could also be carried on mule-back. This was a considerably more accurate weapon with the same maximum range, firing a 20 lb. shell.

Before the war this branch of the R. G. A. was stationed entirely on the frontier of India, and only a few batteries saw service in France.

6 in. 30 cwt. Howitzer: The siege artillery was equipped with another Boer War veteran, the 6 in. 30 cwt. howitzer, first manufactured in 1895. This howitzer fired a shell of approximately 100 lbs., and its maximum range was some 500 yards less than the 18-pounder. It was pulled by a team of twelve heavy draught horses, the weight of the gun and carriage being 3½ tons as compared with the 4½ tons of the 60-pounder. In France early in 1915 mechanical traction was substituted for horses. The howitzer fired from a specially constructed platform consisting of wooden beams like sleepers laid crossways. It took about two hours to level the ground and lay the platform to the middle of which the gun was then screwed down by a spring attachment depending from the carriage. This was a very accurate weapon, but its range was insufficient, and the system of taking up the recoil after firing, antiquated and out-of-date.

6 in. 26 cwt. Howitzer: In consequence, in May, 1915, an entirely new howitzer, known as the 6 in. 26 cwt. was designed and built, with a maximum range of 10,000 yards and a hydraulic recuperative system which rendered it independent of a special platform. This became the standard medium-sized howitzer of the British Army. By the end of the war no less than 1,246 had been issued to the siege artillery and a further 212 to the Allies. The expenditure of 6 in. howitzer ammunition in France was over 22½ million rounds, an average of 10 rounds a minute from August 4th, 1914, to November 11th, 1918.

There were actually eighty-one 6 in. 30 cwt. howitzers available in England at the outbreak of war, but owing to the shortage of trained personnel it was found possible to man only six batteries. These were formed at Plymouth on August 27th, and before the end of September were all landed in France.

6 in. Mark 1: About the middle of October two other siege batteries were improvised at Woolwich. Both were armed with two 6 in. B. L. C. Mark 1 guns, coast defence weapons which had been mounted for the purpose on an elephantine field carriage with traction-engine wheels.

9·2 in. Howitzer: One of these batteries had in its charge the only 9·2 in. howitzer then in existence, the famous 'Mother.' The first equipment of this new siege howitzer had been approved in July, and had just concluded its firing trials when war broke out. On the road this howitzer travelled in three parts, consisting of the barrel, the carriage and cradle, and the bed, each weighing about 4½ tons, mounted on four-wheeled trucks. In action the separate parts were fitted together and bedded in the earth, the whole weighing 15 tons and firing a 290 lbs. shell a maximum range of 10,000 yards (5¾ miles). In later models this range was increased to 12,700 yards (over 7 miles). Four hundred and fifty of these howitzers were issued before the end of the war, and three million rounds of 9·2 in. ammunition were fired.

8 in. Howitzer: About the middle of 1915 an 8 in. howitzer was issued. This is described more particularly in Chapter 4.

12 in. Howitzer: At the end of 1915, 12 in. howitzers began to form part of the equipment of the siege artillery. Some of these were on road mountings similar to those of the 9·2 in. howitzers and others on railway mountings. The weight of the projectile was 850 lbs. and the maximum range 15,600 yards (8½) miles.

6 in. Mark VII: In October of that year the antiquated 6 in. gun was superseded by the Mark VII, a considerably more accurate piece, with a range of about 8¼ miles. Six batteries armed with this gun were landed in France that month.

6 in. Mark XIX: In March, 1917, an improved 6 in. gun was issued, which was known as the 6 in. Mark XIX. This weighed just over 10 tons. The length of the barrel was 18 feet, and its maximum range about 17,000 yards (nearly 10 miles).

Other guns manned by the siege artillery were the 9·2 in., the 12 in., and the 14 in. These were all mounted on railway mountings, and did not begin to appear in France till the middle of 1916. Their range was from 15 to 20 miles.

Ammunition: The ammunition supplied to all guns of lesser calibre than 9·2 in. consisted of shrapnel, H. E., smoke and, from 1916 onwards, gas shell.

H. E. shells were at first manufactured of lyddite but later amatol and tri-nitro-toluene were more frequently used. Picric acid formed the base of the high explosive known as lyddite, and the main difficulty in the production of H. E. shells

14

in the early days of the war was due to the scarcity of this important chemical. Although it is a derivative of that coal tar in which we are so rich, the monopoly of manufacture of this vital product had been allowed to fall into the hands of the enemy.

There is a story that when lyddite was first invented just before the Boer War, a battery of 4·7 in. guns were deputed to test the effectiveness of the new explosive.

Twelve goats were tethered to a barren hillside and the battery at a convenient range opened fire. On the conclusion of the shoot the Major, followed by a large crowd of distinguished spectators, galloped up to see the effect on the goats. Except that their number had been increased to thirteen, they appeared unmoved!

The truth of this story cannot be vouched for, but though the early lyddite shell may have been ineffective, this was not the case with its successor in 1914. Unfortunately, still influenced by the false premise that targets would consist almost wholly of troops in the open, the bulk of the ammunition supplied to the artillery consisted of shrapnel, and it was not until the first Battle of the Somme that the balance was redressed in favour of high explosive.

Shrapnel was extremely effective against personnel in the open. The shell burst over the heads of the enemy infantry and sprayed them with a shower of bullets. It was useless against any form of overhead cover. The accurate shooting of our 18-pounders firing shrapnel was largely responsible for saving the Army of Contemptibles during the retreat from Mons. Howitzers did not normally fire shrapnel.

Smoke shells were used when conditions were bad for observation, to assist in the detection of the burst by the observer. They were also employed to form a smoke screen to conceal the movements of our own troops.

The gulf which existed between the R. G. A. and the R. F. A. was a wider one than that caused by a mere difference of armament. The regular personnel, especially the officers, had, in pre-war days, a hearty brotherly Contempt for all members of the other branch. This amounted, in the case of the more fanatical, to something akin to active dislike. Why and how this absurd situation arose, is lost in the mists of antiquity, but one suspects that that noble animal, the horse, may have had something to do with it. The pre-war field gunner was, on the whole, more interested in horses than in guns. During professional hours horse management and hunting were the chief topics of discussion. His ambition was to attain the honour of a 'jacket,' and, as a horse gunner, to become more completely identified with the cavalry. He was also, as a rule, more moneyed than the garrison gunner, that is to say, he had private means in addition to his pay. The garrison gunner cared for none of these things. He generally lived in forts where horses were superfluous and practically unknown. His business hours were spent in grappling with the technical questions and abstruse calculations pertaining to his craft, and his leisure in sailing and playing games. He described his brother in the R. F. A. as 'a bow-and-arrow merchant who goes in for horse-coping,' and his brother dubbed him 'that scientific Gambardier who wears badly cut breeches.' This fraternal feeling did not altogether cease with the outbreak of war. In spite of the vast number of officers, which soon completely swamped the junior ranks of the artillery, one could still occasionally hear the opprobrious term 'Gambardier' in 18-pounder gun lines, and the derisive word 'pop-gun' applied to those same 18-pounders in the heavy artillery messes.

The R. F. A. had the enormous advantage of belonging to a big family party, the Division. The heavy and siege artillery were usually corps troops. This actually meant that they belonged to nobody, but were moved about from corps front to corps front wherever they were most wanted. There was, however, no real ill feeling except perhaps among the more encrusted of the senior officers, and the whole thing died once and for all during the Gunners' Battle, Ypres, 1917, when all branches of the artillery suffered equally and terribly.

* * * * * * * *

At the end of October, 1914, the authorities at home, urged on by G. H. Q. in France, suddenly awoke to the fact that a larger proportion of howitzers and heavy guns was essential for the successful prosecution of the war. The German field artillery could out-range our own by nearly 3,000 yards. They had a quantity of heavy guns corresponding to the 60-pounders, and in addition they had brought into the field large numbers of heavy howitzers of which the 15 cm. (5·9 in.) and 21 cm. (8·3 in.) were the commonest types. These were used to batter down the forts of Namur, Liege, and Antwerp and later against the field defences, trenches and 'strong points' of the Allies. Introduced into the German army about 1910, these two howitzers fired shells weighing 100 lbs. and 200 lbs. respectively, their maximum range being over 5½ miles.

At this date the number of heavy guns and howitzers with the B. E. F. amounted to eighty-five in all; 14 heavy batteries and 8 siege batteries. It is interesting to compare this with the number of heavy guns and howitzers in France at the end of the war. On November 11th, 1918, the total was 2,215.

It was, therefore, decided to form what almost amounted to a vast new arm—a heavy artillery. Woolwich was allocated as a training ground for the guns, the heavies. Lydd, a desolate spot on the coast of Kent, near Dungeness, fulfilled a similar purpose for the howitzers, the siege. The heavies were to carry out their training on the 4·7 in. but would be armed in the field, as fast as the rate of manufacture would allow, with the 60-pounder. The siege were to train on anything they could lay their hands on, from ancient muzzle-loaders upwards, and would fight with the antiquated 6 in. 30 cwt. howitzer and the modern 9-2 in. howitzer as soon as sufficient of these latter weapons had been constructed.

The following account of the artillery with the B. E. F. at Mons and the Aisne was written by a distinguished gunner officer who commanded a Field Brigade in the Second Division:

When war broke out in 1914 I am very doubtful that the majority of gunner officers, with the first seven Divisions, had any very definite knowledge about the artillery they would be called upon to encounter in the field. We suspected that the German field gun and the light howitzer were most probably inferior to our own in fighting value, and that they possessed a heavier form of field howitzer which we might be called on to face at intervals. The idea of guns and howitzers with a mobile army, of the calibre of the 5-9 in. and upwards, in any considerable quantity, seemed a remote contingency: the difficulties of ammunition supply and mobility would prove too great. The very composition of our own mobile artillery at the outbreak of war fostered this idea, while our allies, the French, at the start, seemed to ignore the howitzer altogether.

On the first day at Mons I was still fairly sure on this point, as on that part of the Second Division front, which formed my outlook on the battle, nothing but field guns and light howitzers were shooting at us.

The next day, when the retreat really began, was my first experience of the 5-9 in. and the anti-aircraft gun, to both of which weapons, at that stage, we had neither rival nor reply. As we were drawn up in defensive positions that morning, covering presumably the retreat of other troops, a large contingent of our cavalry rode across our front, and at the same moment one of our aeroplanes appeared scouting for the enemy. To our surprise a perfect shower of shell bursts appeared around our plane, which fortunately escaped unharmed. The plane was fairly low, I should have guessed it at least 3,000 feet, from which fact we deduced that the fire, from its rapidity and direction, must have come from a gun or guns on a special mounting.

Very shortly afterwards heavy shells, obviously bigger than those of the field gun or light howitzer, began to burst just short of our position. The Germans kept up a slow fire, all of which was short, until we left the position, and I am afraid I complacently considered this as showing he had difficulty in bringing up such a heavy gun, and had not much ammunition with it.

I learnt to know the 5-9 in. better later on, and found that it was by no means the biggest weapon to be used against us in the field.

At the Aisne, in 1914, the morning the crossing was attempted by our troops, my Brigade of Artillery was sent forward from our night quarters to move up in support of the advanced guard Infantry Brigade which Had already marched.

On a dull grey misty morning, about an hour before sunrise, I reached the grassy downland, overlooking the Aisne, and, wheeling to my right, we --trotted along in column of batteries, at close interval, Abe merry rattle of the harness chains and thud of the hooves over the springy turf, reminding me of a 4ft on Salisbury Plain. I used this formation in case the mist lifted suddenly, so that I had only to wheel again right and disappear behind the crest. I found my Brigadier, and took up covering positions near Vieil Arcy. I was sent back to these positions after having crossed in rear of my Division, presumably to act as support, and to cover any troops, in the contingency of their being forced back over the crossing, and here it was I first met real big stuff.

About the second or third day, we were spotted and ranged on by a German aeroplane, and then the fun began. I do not know the exact size of the weapon employed against us, but we were honoured with two hours' slow and solemn strafe. When we returned to the guns again (we were in action in a ploughed field), nothing was injured, but between three of the guns were single shell craters, each occupying the whole of the full interval between two guns. Similar duck ponds to the number of about fifty were all around. I put my adversary down as being about 11 in. calibre. 'I was moved from there to a position overlooking Chavonne and Vailly. Shortly after arriving I had the pleasure of seeing German cavalry, eight abreast, riding along the Chemin des Dames, towards our right flank. This display continued for about three hours. Needless to say they were well beyond reach of my field guns and knew it. In response to my urgent messages, the Divisional Heavy Battery arrived, and put a heavy shell within 100 yards of them but could do no more owing to the range being too great!

Yet another instance of the lack of power, and of ammunition of our artillery equipment. In the far distance beyond Vailly, my attention was drawn to a small square black opening in the slate roof of a prominent house: careful examination assured me it must have been caused by removing one or two slates. I asked my confrere of the Heavies to abolish what was evidently an O. P. giving a magnificent view of our position. He could only spare me ten rounds, and with this at nearly

extreme range he knocked off a corner of the house. Next day every slate was stripped off and it was evident that the occupants had realized their error; but they were safe—we had nothing to throw at them.

An instance of the effect of our Divisional Heavies at tasks within their power, may be quoted here. Shortly after the stabilization of the Aisne battle, the enemy launched an infantry attack on Chavonne. From my O. P. I could plainly see the advancing lines, shoulder to shoulder, about two hundred yards between them, moving forward over a beetroot field. I opened on them joyfully: a real good target at a possible range. I saw the middle two rounds of the bracket, beautifully fused, blow two great gaps in the first line. Before the necessary orders for rapid fire could reach the batteries, our friends the Heavies had banged two lyddite shell fair between the two advancing lines. I found it difficult to be in time even to shell the slowest retreaters, so quickly had those two shell given the order 'Right about turn, double march' evidently in fluent German.

After a week or so our hopes ran high. Our heavy artillery train was coming out, and then we would show them what. And at last it came, dear old dug-out cannon carefully provided to shell Pretoria or was it Sebastopol? It had to be shoved up as far as possible to the front, or the pathetic old things could not carry beyond our front line. Personnel suffered accordingly, and to add to their troubles I heard it was not uncommon .-for our own people to be killed and injured by the defective ammunition and bursting guns of what we Called 'the Noah's Ark Contingent.'

Is it surprising that in the Spring and Summer of 1917 used often to give myself the pleasure, when my work allowed me, of taking an afternoon ride towards the front of the Ypres Salient for the joy of hearing our great howitzer and gun shell whistling and purring over my head, on their way to show Jerry that not only could we take a leaf out of his book, but produce newer and better whole editions?

A Battery Commander's account of one of the early Siege Batteries:

The battery was formed at Woolwich on Thursday, October 8th, 1914. It consisted of "George" and "Mary," two 6 in. B. L. C. Mark I guns and "Mother," the only 9.2 in. howitzer then in existence. Steam tractors were supplied to tow the guns and 5-ton Foden lorries carried the ammunition. These vehicles are familiar to all who take an interest in the transport of beer. They may cheer the thirsty traveller as they snort along our high-grade roads, but they merely provoked profanity, when, laden with five tons of ammunition apiece, they skidded about on the greasy pave on their smooth steel tyres. The drivers, a grimy and somewhat intoxicated crew from Grove Park, were enlisted then and there at the rate of 6s. 9d. per diem, on their own statements that they were experts on road traction engines.

Four days later the battery set sail for France. The march from Havre to Boulogne with this travelling circus was a nightmare. One might start with intervals of ten yards from nose to tail but the yards soon became miles. Steam engines, it appeared, required watering every few miles, and the country was strewn with Foden wagons falling out to water at *estaminets*. At every halt the village elders gathered round to wonder and admire. France was saved! *Vivent les Alliésa bas les Boches!*

One touching little incident remains in my mind. It was on a fine Sunday morning. A young girl came out of a village shop as we approached, and shyly presented each officer with a combined pen and pencil, and every man with a piece of chocolate. I have my pen and pencil still.

The guns were eventually sent up to the front separately, "George" being the first to leave Boulogne. "Mother" came into action for the first time at La Gouture on October 31st where extraordinary precautions were taken for her safety, an armed infantry guard and an anti-aircraft section being detailed to protect her. Everybody who could came to inspect this new monster, including, on November 18th, the Prince of Wales.

Our early efforts at shooting with these Gargantuan weapons and the cumbrous pre-war telephone and observation of fire instruments, need not be dwelt upon. Time shrapnel drove us nearly to despair. Needless to say, we were always required to shoot at extreme ranges, and it was a common occurrence for two successive rounds fired with the same fuse and elevation to burst 700 yards apart!

Chapter 1

1914

On a lovely summer's evening in late august, 1914, a very youthful gunner subaltern might have been seen pacing up and down the cliffs which hide the battery in front of Tynemouth Castle. Before him were two long snake-like 6 in. guns peering out to sea over the tops of their emplacements, behind were the tall ruins of the old castle, a magnificent mark for enemy gunners, and to his immediate right was the mouth of the river Tyne, with its two long piers running out to form the harbour. There was nothing particularly remarkable about this young officer except that he was weeping silently and bitterly. Had any casual passer-by chanced to observe this unusual and very un-English behaviour, and ventured to question its cause he would doubtless have been told to 'shut up for God's sake,' or received some even cruder and equally unsatisfying reply. The cause of the trouble lay too deep for human sympathy. The news of the Retreat from Mons had just come in. Many of our subaltern's school and 'shop' friends had been there and he had not. He had missed the whole war, which would certainly be over by Christmas, if not before. The whole of his life's work was wasted. All those examinations, which hang like the sword of Damocles over the regardless head of Youth, had been successfully circumvented, and now, having attained his life's ambition, His Majesty's Commission, it was only to be shut up in this God-forsaken fort, teaching God-forsaken Territorials bow to shoot at imaginary submarines, which always turned out to be sea-gulls. It was too bitter. Our subaltern, whose name was Shadbolt, could think of nothing adequate in words or deeds to cope with the situation. Indeed, those first three months cooped up in a Coast Defence fort on the East Coast were trying ones to officers and men alike. All those who could be spared were taken at once to form new heavy batteries elsewhere or as reinforcements to those already in France. Their place had been taken by Territorials who, excellent fellows, and very keen, were only partially trained, and naturally took some time to become acclimatised. Every day and night there were rumours of invasions and raids and big fleet actions in the North Sea. Enemy submarines were always supposed to be lurking at the very mouth of the Tyne. Guns were continuously manned, searchlights swept the sea from dusk to dawn, and everyone was prepared to fight to the last to save England from immediate invasion. Indeed, one elderly officer, who should have known better, was never seen without his sword and two loaded revolvers.

Finally there was the Examination Service. This consisted of an Examination vessel at the mouth of the harbour, which was in close touch with the Examination battery, two 6 in. guns at the fort. Both were equipped with a special signal code which changed every two hours. Any vessel, of whatever nationality, size, or description, which attempted to enter the harbour, was accosted by the Examination vessel, boarded and examined, and if found all correct, supplied with the special signal. She was then permitted to enter the harbour without molestation by the battery. Should, however, any vessel attempt to enter without the signal, or flying an incorrect signal, then the officer on duty had strict orders to fire a round of common shell (one containing no high explosive) across her bows, followed by a round of H. E. into her hull should she still rashly continue to proceed.

In this connection an incident occurred which was destined to have a profound effect on Shadbolt's future fortunes. One rough and boisterous Sunday afternoon in November he was on duty in the little wooden signallers' hut at the top of the cliff, which served as look-out post for the officer in charge of the Examination battery. There was a good deal of shipping outside the harbour, but most of it was waiting for the tide to turn before venturing in. The gun crews were in their concrete dugouts below the guns playing cards and yarning. Shadbolt was sitting over the oil-stove wishing his relief would appear and he could go in to tea. Suddenly an excited signaller, who had been staring intently through his telescope reported 'Ship entering the 'arbour, sir, flying incorrect signals.' Snatching the telescope from his hand Shadbolt observed a big freighter, the S. S. *Kenilworth,* flying the signals of the previous hour, making straight for the harbour mouth. He knew the *Kenilworth* well. She was an English ship. It was obvious that she had obtained the correct signal earlier in the day and had then waited for high tide. Meanwhile the signal was changed, and there she was coming in flying the wrong one. Shadbolt's orders were quite implicit. Without hesitation he seized a megaphone and rushing out into the storm gave the order 'Action.' It was the work of less than a minute to point out the target, give the necessary deflection to cause the shell to fall well in front of the ship's bows, and order fire. Unfortunately Gunner Smith, the layer, a conscientious and painstaking though somewhat slow-witted individual, had also been thinking of his tea. The swift transition from such ethereal flights of fancy to the cold and sober world of fact upset him. He forgot to put on that deflection. The first round sailed just over the *Kenilworth's* bridge and landed with a splash about a hundred yards beyond the target—— The feelings of the *Kenilworth's* patriotic skipper at this outrage have never been made public, but he was literally between the devil, as represented by Gunner Smith, and the deep sea. The gale was too strong to allow of any turning back. He was almost at the harbour's mouth and must go on.

Though failing to appreciate the skipper's quandary, Shadbolt was grappling with a serious enough problem of his own, those implicit orders 'should a ship continue to approach after the first round, she was to be sunk by gun-fire.' Here was an English ship, to that he could swear, but supposing there was something wrong. He decided to compromise by firing another round across her bows. Gunner Smith made no mistake about the deflection this time. He put it on and a bit more for luck. The *Kenilworth* was now so near the mouth of the harbour that the shell cleared the further pier-head by a miracle, ricocheted in the sea beyond and landed in the roof of an old woman's cottage about two miles down the coast. Luckily, being a common shell, it could not explode, but contented itself with making a neat hole in the kitchen floor, and causing alarmist rumours of a heavy German bombardment on unprotected civilians.

At this critical juncture the relief appeared, accompanied by a senior officer, who had come down to see what all the firing was about. Hastily explaining the situation, Shadbolt fled for the mess. Hardly, however, had the first piece of hot-buttered toast disappeared, when the sound of rockets and other signals of distress brought him outside again. The distraught Captain of the *Kenilworth,* not daring to come on, and unable to turn back, had piled his ship on the rocks below the battery.

The sequel to this story took place somewhere in France about seven months later. Shadbolt had been wounded, but not badly enough to constitute a 'blighty' one. After a week in hospital he had returned to the battery, which was being frequently shelled, and things were pretty black from Shadbolt's point of view, when a telegram arrived from H. Q., '2nd Lt. Shadbolt will return to U. K. immediately and report to War Office re sinking of S.S. *Kenilworth.*'

But life on Examination duty was not always so exciting. Long nights were spent by tired subalterns and sleepy signallers gazing into the beams of the searchlights, brewing hot cocoa over the oil-stove, and longing for the dawn. Very occasionally and always in the middle of the night, a gun would go off by itself. This mysterious and disturbing occurrence, disturbing at least for those who were asleep in the barracks behind the castle, could never be satisfactorily accounted for. Should a round be fired and a second one loaded, it was not possible to extricate the second shell from the bore except by firing, and test calls for action were always given two or three times a night to make sure that gun crews were alert and ready. What probably happened was that Gunner Smith, disturbed from semi-slumber by a sudden call, rushed up on the emplacement and pulled the trigger of the loaded gun before his mind had fully wakened to reality. Again, the remarkable resemblance of a sea-gull or a piece of wreckage floating on the water to an enemy periscope may have proved the undoing of excitable and inexperienced young officers.

These began to flow in as September merged into October, in a steady stream, and it was found possible to relieve some of the older hands from continuous watch-keeping and to post them to other duties. One day suddenly Shadbolt found himself in charge of an anti-aircraft gun with crew complete, guarding the oil-tanks on the other side of the river. This gun deserves special mention as a unique weapon to be met only in musical comedy or in the very early days of the war. It consisted of a pom-pom, which had seen good service in the Boer War, mounted on a special mounting to enable it to deal with Zeppelins and other birds of prey. The little shells were loaded from a belt, like a machine gun, and the whole contrivance was fired by the light of nature over open sights. There were no bothering calculations as to height, range, and speed of target. Nobody had ever seen it fired. Nobody ever did. The crew consisted of a bombardier, four men and a Labrador retriever, this last the personal property of Shadbolt. They lived in some discomfort, but in perfect peace and tranquillity, in a little shed on the wharf where the oil-tanks were situated. The only excitement took place about twice a week when the torpedo destroyers came in to refuel. At first this was also the only occasion when Shadbolt got a meal which showed any variation from ration stew and coal dust served on a tin plate. Later on the complete absence of hostile aircraft encouraged him to seek more commodious quarters, and he encamped in the Board Room of the Tyneside Commissioners about a hundred yards from the wharf. Here he was able to do his own cooking on the Commissioners' open fire-place. Breakfast was a great success, porridge, eggs and bacon, and hot toast all being comparatively simple from a culinary point of view. The other meals, however, were not so easy, especially as the Commissioners seemed always to have a board-meeting about lunch time, necessitating striking camp and pushing everything hurriedly, including the retriever, into the adjoining office. This peaceful existence continued for a month when the whole party was suddenly ordered back to the castle.

Early in November the first four of the new siege batteries mobilised at Lydd, and wild with delight and martial ardour, Shadbolt found himself among them. They were composed entirely of Regular troops, the men being the pick of the Coast Defence stations, and a finer collection, physically, it would have been hard to find. The officers were also all Regulars, with the exception of a subaltern from the special Reserve in Shad-bolt's battery, whose name was Alington. This officer, who shortly afterwards took a Regular commission, was known among the men as 'Legs' Eleven' on account of his long legs and inordinate length of stride. The men's quarters and the officers' mess, being pre-war, were fairly comfortable, but Lydd itself was the abomination of desolation, especially in winter. Perched on a shingly spit of land about a mile inland from Dungeness, it was exposed to all the winds that blew. Training was carried on in bitter cold, wintry weather, aggravated by driving blasts of rain and sleet. Numbed fingers fumbled with directors, dial sights and other instruments of fire: frozen brains grappled with range tables. Yet everybody was happy! Would they not be in France by Christmas? And then the war would soon be over. They would blow the Hun off the face of the map.

As the war years rolled on, and more and more embryo batteries poured into Lydd for their final training, Shadbolt, from the comparative warmth and comfort of a dug-out in France, often pitied its poor denizens struggling to carry on without the assistance of 'that first, fine careless rapture.'

In those early days, much time was spent learning to shoot with obsolete weapons. As the elementary principles of gunnery apply regardless of the period and nature of the armament, this time was not so much time wasted as would at first sight appear. In addition to 15-pounders and 5 in. muzzle loaders, two nineteenth century veterans belonging to an enemy country were wakened from their long sleep and pressed into service. The 9-45 in. howitzer or Quarter-to-Ten, as it was always called, had been manufactured at Skoda in Austria about 1890. The British Government purchased eight of these in 1900, and shipped them to South Africa in packing cases marked 'pianos.' They were intended to take part in the siege of Pretoria, but, arriving too late, were eventually shipped home to England without firing a round. Owing to their foreign manufacture, the breech on these weapons opened the opposite way to that on all British guns, from right to left, instead of from left to right. This caused great consternation amongst the drill experts, and the whole of the gun-drill had to be altered especially for them. The Quarter-to-Ten was mounted on a fixed platform bedded deep in the ground. To dismount these two Brobdingnagian antiques and mount them again, a quarter of a mile away, took Shadbolt's battery the whole of one winter's night from dusk to dawn.

Training proceeded apace, and included, in addition to gun-drill and the actual shooting on the ranges, lessons in the construction of gun-pits and dug-outs, route marches, physical training, lectures on gunnery and classes for specialists such as signallers, observers, gun-layers and B. C. A's. The Battery Commander's Assistant, or more shortly B. C. A. was a highly trained N. C. O. specially selected for his superior intelligence, who assisted the Battery Commander in working out calculations, tabulated them on completion, and was generally responsible for all maps, range tables, and technical instruments. The officers were taught their duties as section commanders, and were instructed in map reading, reconnaissance work, the collection and reporting of information, and the working out of targets and lines of fire.

Life, however, was not all work. In the evenings a very boisterous and happy family met in the mess and indulged in snooker, sing-songs, cock-fighting and other - sports common to British officers' messes the world over. In addition to the permanent camp staff there were eight officers from each battery, two R. F. C. officers, two or three senior officers home from the front with hair-raising stories of Mons and the Marne, and one cavalry man turned balloonatic. One night, at the close of dinner, the Mess President announced that 2nd Lt. Shadbolt would stand port all round for making a bet with his neighbour that the war would be over by Christmas. Poor Shadbolt looked a bit blue as forty odd ports meant nearly a week's pay, but as, later on, most of the recipients seemed to think it incumbent on them to stand the donor one back, life once more resumed its roseate hue, and the evening ended more riotously than ever. When finally Christmas did arrive, everyone, with the exception of the balloonatic, was still at Lydd, and hasty preparations were made to spend the festive season appropriately. No leave to sleep away was given, so after making the usual devastating round of visits to men's dinners and assimilating the consequent jorums of port and beer, the younger officers got together and decided to hire cars with a view to making a strategic attack on the Metropole at Folkestone. Later in the day this was carried out according to plan. A dance was in progress at the hotel, and there seemed to be a shortage of men. About three o'clock the following morning a distracted senior subaltern was still vainly endeavouring to round up his reluctant flock for the cold and dismal journey back to Lydd. The occasion was impressed on Shadbolt's mind by the fact that he lost his Sam Browne. Whether some hero-worshipping damsel stole it for a souvenir or whether the manager impounded it in part payment of his account he never discovered.

To the thoughtful reader anxious to obtain some general impression of the atmosphere of the home front during those early days, or dimly remembering perhaps his own very different sensations, this light-hearted way of taking the war may seem strange. It should, however, be remembered that, unlike every other formation of the New Army, the heavy and siege artillery was at first composed entirely of Regular soldiers. To these men the outbreak of war and the consequent need of heavy guns signified at long last the fulfilment of their destiny. Most of the older hands had spent long and weary years sweltering or freezing in coast defence forts at places like Singapore or Spike Island. To them, in those bygone days, the prospect of war had meant no release from their bondage, no opportunities for promotion and honour. Most of them had felt that in any case coast defence duty was somewhat of an anachronism. Provided the Navy were intact, there was no need for coast defence. Should the Navy be defeated, coast defence, as represented by widely scattered fortresses, would be of little or no use against a determined enemy. Now all that was forgotten. Here was a definite and crying need, which they, as fully-trained gunners, were alone able to supply. Here was opportunity in full measure, not only for mere personal honour and advancement, but to take their share in serving England at the most critical hour of her history.

CHAPTER 2

Festubert—1915

To the men in Flanders, that first long winter of 1914-1915 was the most terrible of all. Their trenches were waterlogged for want of suitable material to build and drain them, their reliefs were few and far between for want of men, their efforts to keep the enemy in check were rendered abortive for want of artillery support. All day long they were shelled with 'whizz-bangs' and 'woolly bears,' 'coal-boxes' and 'black Marias,' but nothing ever went back. The Field Artillery had no ammunition, the heavy artillery had no guns. The poor battered infantry were paying England's usual penalty, one which has a precedent in every war in her history, the penalty of being unprepared.

Meanwhile those at home were straining every nerve to repair that tragic lack. Our four siege batteries at Lydd were trained and ready to the last field dressing. Only one thing was wanting—guns. Other batteries were being formed and mobilised in Coast Defence stations all over the country, waiting to proceed to Lydd as soon as room should be made for them by the departure of the first four. Finally, in February, the long-awaited orders were received. Two batteries, armed with 9-2 in. howitzers were to embark for France immediately, and two, armed with 6 in. howitzers were to proceed to Portsmouth, there to await the final collection of their stores and guns before sailing.

It now transpired that the real cause of the delay in sending the 6 in. howitzers overseas was the vexed question of traction and transport. A specially constructed lorry with a four-wheel drive had been devised to pull the gun and carry the gun's crew. Other lorries were to carry the ammunition, and the vast amount of technical stores considered necessary to keep a siege battery continually in action in the field. The experiments with the F. W. D.'s., as these special lorries were called, had not yet been completed. They were carried out then and there on the Portsmouth Downs, and this mode of traction proved eminently satisfactory. In countries with good and sufficient roads, such as were fought over on the Western Front, the F. W. D.'s were infinitely superior in speed and mobility to the old-fashioned teams of cart horses. The 60-pounders, however, kept to their horses, and occasionally had the doubtful satisfaction of lending them to their tractor-driven brethren in order to help them out of the mud, as after heavy rain the tractors were helpless off the road.

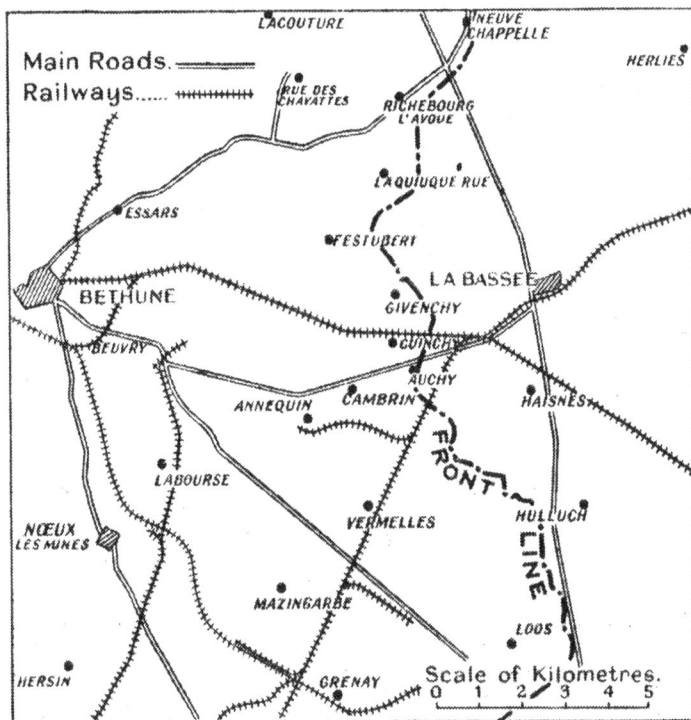

Shadbolt once saw this situation reversed when a 60-pounder got so stuck in a ploughed field on the Somme that it took seven caterpillar-tractors hooked on in tandem to extract it. The caterpillar was the ungainly monster, not unlike a steam-roller with caterpillar wheels substituted for rollers, which formed the mode of traction for all siege artillery of larger calibre than the 6 in. howitzer (with the exception of those on railway mountings).

All forms of traction for the siege artillery, caterpillars, F.W.D.'s and lorries, were in charge of the A.S.C., who supplied the necessary drivers and effected all the repairs. This arrangement was not an entirely satisfactory one from the point of view of the artillery. It meant that a Battery Commander had no direct control over his own power of movement. It was true that an A. S. C. subaltern was attached to each battery nominally under the orders of the B. C., but in practice this did not amount to a great deal. In the line the lorry park, for obvious reasons, was situated a long way in rear of the battery. Lorries were wanted by all sorts of formations for all kinds of jobs, and it was only in the nature of things that they should sometimes be commandeered by local deities for their own particular ends. Nor was it always easy for the A. S. C. to decide the relative importance of a battery's needs and those of higher formations. But on the whole, they worked wholeheartedly and loyally for the artillery, and the R. G. A. owe them a very deep debt of gratitude.

At last all was ready and our two batteries, complete with lorries, guns, ammunition and enough baggage and impedimenta to do justice to the Queen of Sheba on a state visit to King Solomon, set sail for France. The Germans must have had news of this imposing armament, for the ship containing the guns was but a few hours out from Avonmouth when the dreaded periscope of a submarine was sighted. Undaunted, the subaltern in charge pulled a 6 in. howitzer out of the hold, and proceeded to open fire. Imagine trying to hit an active trout in a pond by lobbing at it with a cricket ball! No shot fell within a quarter of a mile of the submarine, but this strange combat went on for nearly two hours. For some reason, at the end of this period the submarine gave up the chase and was no more seen.

Three days after landing at Rouen the two batteries, now formed into a brigade, proceeded by road to Aire. After a further week's delay, orders were received to occupy positions in the line near Festubert. Moving into a battery position at night within a mile of the front line was always an unpleasant, if not necessarily a hazardous undertaking, but on this occasion it was carried out without incident. The long column of lorries and guns, with all lamps doused, crawled up the narrow pave road from Bethune in the darkness. Presently they saw for the first time that amazing firework display of Very lights which every night from dusk to dawn, from Switzerland to the sea, illuminated the Western front. There was little or no gunfire, but the silence was broken by the occasional rat-tat of a machine-gun or the crack of a solitary rifle. The general effect might be compared to that of a life-size picture by Dore of Dante's approach to Inferno. The waving arms of a shattered tree, the derelict remains of a sightless house, appeared and disappeared in the fitful light of the distant flares. These flares were sparks thrown up from the fires of hell, and the crackle of rifle fire was the shrivelling in the furnace of the bones of the damned. At one point the road was blocked by infantry coming out on relief, and a sergeant of the Loamshires, out since Mons, spent an enjoyable two minutes regaling the newcomers with a complete list of the battalion casualties since that date.

The position taken up was in an orchard off the Rue de Chevattes, near Richebourg. There was only room for two guns, so the other two went into action about 50 yards further down the road. The first two, under Captain Gregory, led an isolated but extremely strenuous existence in the orchard. Gregory was an old mountain gunner, who had seen some active service on the frontier, a small man with a large personality, brimful of energy, and with Spartan ideas about discipline and the proper conduct of a war. He lived in a pair of large rubber thigh boots and went to bed at night under a bivouac on the ground, the rubber boots, with his feet in them, sticking out from under the flap.

The guns were always manned at dawn. From then onwards every man was kept hard at it, sorting ammunition, polishing breech-blocks, digging dug-outs, doing gun-drill, quite apart from the actual firing. All meals were eaten off a tin plate, balanced precariously on the knees, and consisted of bully beef and biscuits, varied by ration stew as provided for the troops by a benevolent Government. It was considered extremely unsoldierlike for an officer to supplement these rations with luxuries from home or the local canteen. These views did not, however, appeal to the sybarites Alington and Shadbolt, and they made unavailing efforts to soften the heart of that grim soldier, Gregory, and to induce him to eat his food off a table, take his boots off at night and share the amenities of the farm cart lined with straw where the two subalterns slept side by side like the Babes in the Wood.

This question of comfort in the line was ever afterwards one to which Shadbolt gave his particular attention. He took the view that as the gunners were nearly always in the line, and seldom, if ever, went out on rest like the infantry, it was up to them to make their permanent home as comfortable as the conditions would allow. A man's efficiency was not improved, but actually impaired, by undergoing unnecessary discomforts. Even Shadbolt, however, could not live up to the high standard of a certain Corps Commander, who in 1917 came to inspect a siege battery in the line near Ypres. After being shown the guns, the dug-outs, the B.C. post, the telephone exchange, and even the latrines, the Great Man said, 'And now I should like to see the men's dining-room.'

Batteries, of course, were always being moved from one part of the line to another. No sooner had they settled in and got themselves really comfortable than orders came from headquarters for a move, and the whole business of home-making had to be gone through again. Here the garrison gunner had a big pull over other units, as, like the well-known denizen of the garden, he carried his house on his back. When a siege battery moved, the lorries would be packed with chairs, tables, wire beds and other furniture, in addition to the legitimate stores. This was strictly against orders, but the wise Battery Commander always turned a blind eye to this house-moving, provided the golden rule was not broken, comfort without impairment of efficiency.

This is really a corollary to Napoleon's maxim, 'An army marches upon its stomach.'

The above panegyric on comfort and its relation to efficiency in war should not lead the reader to deduce that the heavy artillery was always comfortable. Far from it. This will be made abundantly clear if he has the patience to pursue this history a little further.

Another mountain gunner of the old school was the Colonel of the Brigade. He was entirely without fear, and if he had been allowed his own way would, without doubt, have put all his 6 in. howitzers into the frontline trench, there to blow the opposing enemy trench sky high like a stockade of savages in the jungle. The observation post (O.P.) at that period was a house on the Rue de Bois about 400 yards from the German front line. Half the side of the house facing the enemy was intact, the other half was completely blown off leaving the upper rooms exposed. Shadbolt was on duty one morning observing from the intact side of the house, when the Colonel came up and suggested they might get a better view from the exposed upper room. He accordingly strolled upstairs followed by the reluctant subaltern, and there remained erect, manoeuvring a telescope in full view of the whole German Army. After five or six minutes, during which Shadbolt felt as if he were standing naked before a firing squad, he wandered tranquilly down again and proceeded on his way. As usually happened on these occasions, the Germans turned belated but accurate shell-fire on the spot where the gallant old Colonel had been, so that those who were left behind had to suffer for his indiscretion.

Shortly afterwards the Brigade suffered its first casualty in the loss of the subaltern on duty at this very O. P. The Colonel continued on his foolhardy course, utterly regardless of his life or safety, was promoted to Brigadier-General a year later, and then, whilst exposing himself more recklessly than usual, was killed by a wandering bullet.

On May 9th, the Brigade took part in the Battle of Festubert. The night before Alington and Shadbolt slept lightly and uneasily in their farm cart. About an hour before dawn they rose in the darkness and crept shivering on to their guns. Except for an occasional rifle shot, the front was deathly quiet, and one could plainly hear men stumbling about and shouting in the neighbouring fields as, by the fitful lantern-light, they prepared their monstrous gods for the coming day.

Suddenly there was a deafening crack, followed by four stabbing flashes of flame. The 18-pounder battery behind had opened fire. As if this were the signal, every battery on the front crashed into a thunderous accompaniment, and the whole earth seemed to shake to the blasting roar of their guns. Shadbolt's first battle had begun. In the half light behind the gun he watched the mechanical feeding of an insatiable monster by its statuesque slaves, their grey, unshaven faces contorted by the flickering gun-fire into something evil and unearthly. This diabolic illusion was increased by their continual ramming and stoking, their tireless activity, and their silence. Across the orchard the men on Alington's gun were working with the same precise and deadly concentration. Through the trees he could see his friend's long legs moving restlessly to and fro, as he checked the sights and ammunition, and superintended the working of his detachment.

The whole of that bright May day this devil's work went on, and in the evening its first results appeared in the shape of a few shaken-looking prisoners in muddy field grey, who crept in listless batches down the road behind the battery position. The gunners crowded round them demanding 'Souvenir,' the only word common to all the nations at war. Each man returned with a helmet, the old German *pickel-haube*, a set of buttons, a belt, or a haversack. One wondered if those poor prisoners would retain even their clothes by the time they arrived in rear.

The next day Shadbolt was sent forward to observe from a captured German trench. Taking with him his batman, Gunner Langmead, and two signallers, he threaded his way through a maze of battered trenches. Sandbags and dead bodies lay jumbled there in wild confusion, as if some petulant giant, growing tired of play, had thrown down his broken toys in heaps. Finally they arrived in a little trench so choked with dead and so void of all semblance of a parapet, that it had been left unoccupied by our troops. Sandbagging up one corner of this, Shadbolt and the signallers settled down to the day's work, whilst the cherubic-faced batman set off on the inevitable souvenir hunt. He had just left when the enemy began a tremendous bombardment, the exact centre of which seemed to be situated on their isolated and defenceless little post. Shells were bursting with thundering concussions in front and in rear, to the right and to the left and in the air above, when the Major rang up from the battery to inquire what was happening, and whether a counter-attack was impending. These were points which Shadbolt would gladly have been clear about himself, as he knew that between him and the enemy, a few hundred yards away, there was only one tired company of Coldstream Guards in a hastily thrown up trench. 'You must go and find the infantry O. C., ask what's happening, and what we can do to help.' This meant a hundred and fifty yards mostly over the open. At school Shadbolt had won a cup for the quarter-mile, but he beat his own record that day. Arriving panting and splashed with mud, he was informed by a bored sentry that the officers were having lunch about two bays down the trench, and as he rounded the next traverse he caught the words 'Fruit salad, m'lord.' Apparently quite unmoved by the activities of the enemy, they asked him to lunch, and suggested that, when things had quieted down, he should shoot up a machine gun which was worrying them. Declining the friendly invitation, he only stayed to locate the offending machine gun, and then bolted back to reassure the Major.

A quarter of an hour later when the bombardment had died down to scattered shelling, in staggered Master Langmead, absolutely covered with *pickel-haubes*, sword-bayonets, and other trophies of war. 'Please sir, I'm sorry I've been away so long, but I've brought you this ring which I got orf a dead orficer's finger.'

In the evening, after Shadbolt had dealt faithfully with the machine-gun, the enemy put down another fierce 'hate.' The little party laden with telephones, reels of wire, rifles, kit, spare food, and Langmead's souvenirs, sallied out as soon as it seemed safe, and made a dive for the trench behind. This was packed with Canadians waiting, with bayonets fixed and set faces, to make another attack. There followed another sprint to a third trench and then a fourth. Suddenly the air was torn with the crackling rattle of musketry and machine-guns. Up got the Canadians in front and in the far distance Shadbolt thought he saw grey forms hurrying eastwards.

Borne down with heat and the weight of the telephone reels there was still trench after trench to be passed, all crowded with anxious, waiting men from whom the words 'Canadians attacking, Germans running,' brought a smile of relief and a muttered 'Thank Gawd, sir, for that.' And so wearily home, meeting one of the fresh Highland battalions from England marching up to relieve the Coldstreams. They looked grim and determined enough. Shadbolt had known one of the Company Commanders at home and shouted him a cheery greeting, but he only stared blankly and made no reply.

Early in June the battery moved to Annequin, where a

whole month was spent without firing a round. Every effort had been made by those at home to supply the much-needed ammunition for Neuve Chapelle and Festubert. At the last-named battle some of the 6 in. shells were stencilled April 24th showing that no time was wasted between the factory and the gun. Actually, since the beginning of the war about 49,000 rounds had been shipped to France by this date. This compares with 38,000 a month for the first six months of 1916, 290,000 a month during the Battle of the Somme, 840,000 a month throughout 1917, and over a million a month in 1918.

The effect of these early battles was to shoot away all the available supply, and for some months after Festubert all siege batteries were reduced to a maximum of twelve rounds a day. At that time the only ammunition supplied to these batteries was some 6 in. gun shell from Gibraltar, which had been condemned as unserviceable in the piping times of peace. To ensure safety these were fired by means of a specially long lanyard, all the gun's crew being ordered out of the gun-pit except the hero who pulled the string. A premature occurred in a neighbouring battery, which blew the whole of the front of the barrel off. But owing to the care that was taken when firing*these condemned shells no casualties occurred. Whether they caused any casualties amongst the enemy is also an open question.

A few 6 in. shrapnel were also issued, but it was found quite impossible to persuade them to burst at the right spot in the path of their trajectory. This is, of course, just before they reach the ground so that the shrapnel bullets spray out like the drops from a watering can. Fired from the howitzers they usually burst about a quarter of a mile up in the air, or on the ground, or quite frequently not at all.

Time hung very heavily for officers and men alike. Books and newspapers were in great demand, and the arrival of the mail from home was the outstanding event of the day. The captain sketched, the subalterns loafed and read, and the gunners played 'house' all day. This is a gambling card game, much beloved by the troops, and consists in betting on the face value of the cards dealt out to each player. Part of a second pack is then dealt, the dealer in a sing-song voice calling out the values, most of which have special names. On a hot afternoon, half asleep under a gun tarpaulin, Shadbolt and Alington listened to the droning, unceasing chant 'Clicketty Click, Number Seven, Kelly's Eye, Legs' Eleven, Number Nine, Top o' the House,' while in the distance a regular whine and bang indicated that the enemy gunners were getting rid of their daily allotment. Nearby, a battery of French 75's, like irritated terriers, would occasionally reply with a spurt of angry yapping, but elsewhere from the British positions all was quiet.

Shadbolt visited the French battery once or twice, and was much impressed by their methods. He never found more than four men in the battery position, one to each gun, though there must have been others hidden away somewhere. On his first visit he was accosted by a friendly-looking tramp in odds and ends of soiled uniform, who appeared to be the only inhabitant. This individual turned out to be a sergeant and, finding that the visitor understood French and was also a gunner, was only too delighted to show him round and to describe the inner workings. After an exhaustive inspection of the whole battery he inquired whether *'Monsieur le Capitaine'* would like to fire a round at the *'sale Boche.'* Shadbolt said he would. Without further ceremony the Frenchman pushed a round into the bore and told him to shoot. Thereupon he banged into the blue, shook hands with his gallant ally, and departed, still without seeing another soul. Shadbolt could not help contrasting this with the methods employed in his own battery, where the procedure of firing involved a solemn ritual including an officer and six acolytes per gun, and attendant High Priests standing round with range tables and telephones.

The O. P. for the Annequin position was situated in the wing of a large distillery 'n the support line. At various times this had been occupied as an O. P. by every battery in the British Army as well as by the French and Germans in 1914. In the vast cellar lived the signallers and telephone exchanges of no less than five batteries. They had made themselves comfortable with lanterns and stoves, broken arm-chairs, old French beds, and a piano. The first night that Shadbolt arrived the Germans were putting up their usual evening hate on the village behind. The noise of bursting enemy shells was loud and continuous, but the only retaliation from the British lines was 'Hold your hand out, you Naughty Boy,' played, to an accompaniment of much laughter and shouting, on the cellar piano. He decided to sleep upstairs, where the advantages of a large double-bed and plenty of fresh air seemed to outweigh the possible disadvantages of a wandering whizz-bang or a spent rifle bullet. One wall of his bedroom had been blown away and he looked straight down a long vista of ruined rooms on which the flarelights from the trenches cast flickering, fantastic shadows. The ghosts of all the nations, who had fought and died in this place, crept and peered and prowled. Every so often a brick would fall or a bomb go off, and they would stop and listen—Shadbolt was connected by a speaking tube to the cellar, but it seemed hardly in keeping with his dignity as a British officer to order Gunner Langmead up to keep him company.

Another O. P. was in a ruined house in Cuinchy, just off the La Bassee road. One sultry Sunday afternoon when all else was 'quiet on the Western Front' the enemy began methodically to shell the building with 5.9 in.'s. Shadbolt and a subaltern from another battery who were both on duty, thought it best to retire to a small sandbag dug-out at the back. They stood at the entrance to the dug-out, which was splinter proof and no more, and watched the performance with professional interest. In the stillness one could hear the German howitzer fire, followed by the long-drawn whine of the approaching shell, and the shattering burst as it landed on a house or a garden wall. They counted the overs and shorts, and the rights and lefts and were presently joined by Saunders from Shadbolt's battery, who had come up to repair the telephone wire which had been cut by the shelling. Suddenly one shell seemed to be coming much closer, and Shadbolt felt a sharp pain in his leg as he dived with the others for the mouth of the dug-out. The blast of the explosion knocked him flat, and when he staggered to his feet he found both the others, covered with mud and blood, moaning on the ground. Binding them up as well as he could, he then discovered that a small splinter had severed a muscle in his thigh, that the telephone wires were again cut, and that the enemy had gone to gun-fire, that is, having found the range slowly and methodically with one gun, he was now firing the whole battery as hard and as fast as he could.

It seemed as if the rocking dug-out would certainly collapse on them with the mere force of the explosions. Saunders was unconscious, but the other subaltern, who was badly hit, kept crying for help in a piteous way. There was nothing to be done but wait. After what seemed to be an eternity, but was in reality not more than ten or fifteen minutes, a figure appeared at the doorway and a quiet voice said 'Are any of you fellows alive?' It was the Colonel. It appeared that a hysterical signaller had run the whole way down to the battery and reported that three officers had been killed and the O. P. destroyed. Whereupon the Colonel, who happened to be in the position, had calmly walked up through the shelling to see for himself, whilst an ambulance was sent for by telephone.

There followed for Shadbolt a week of peace in a casualty clearing station some miles behind Bethune, a week spent mostly in an old walled garden reading books and writing letters. After that, being fit to hobble and the brigade short of officers owing to the loss of the two subalterns, he returned to duty.

The effect of shell-fire on the mind is a cumulative one. When Shadbolt and his companions first landed in France, coming under shell-fire did not immediately produce in them a feeling of intense terror or an acute realisation of its dangers. On the contrary, it was regarded as an interesting and exciting experience, with an element of danger to others, but not to anyone so divinely favoured as themselves. The relief at finding they were not afraid after all, induced a kind of foolhardy recklessness which was generally the hall-mark of the new-comer to war. As the novelty and excitement wore off, and the horrors of experience impressed themselves on the mind, the fear of death and disablement became ever-present realities. It was then that the imaginative man conquered his shaking limbs and with panic in his heart performed deeds, which, though insignificant in themselves, were deeds of daily, nay, hourly heroism.

This strain of never-ceasing effort to conquer the imagination wore men down more surely than hardship and wounds. The artillery suffered perhaps more continuously than the infantry, for they were always in the line. On the other hand this was more than counter-balanced by the fact that the infantry had a far worse time while they were actually in the trenches.

On his return from hospital, Shadbolt knew that he had lost that first light-hearted feeling of personal invulnerability. This was borne in on him very forcibly a week or so later, when the battery was heavily shelled, two guns were completely knocked out, and he was caught in his bath, a situation in which one feels the extreme of human defencelessness. A company of infantry, who were resting in the village, took refuge in the battery dug-outs and lost twenty-four killed and forty-two wounded. The losses in the battery were miraculously small, as so accurate was the German gunnery that every shell fell in the right section, whilst the two guns of the left were untouched. The Major reported to H. Q. that he thought he knew the location of the German battery, and was promptly ordered by the Colonel to engage it at once with his remaining two guns. The rest of the front was utterly quiet. Save for the unusual spectacle of a duel *à outrance* between a German and a British battery, there might have been no war in Flanders. The German had the advantage of having got the range by aeroplane, and of having already destroyed half his opponent's armament. The Britisher was firing gallantly and probably entirely ineffectually into space.

In the evening, when the casualties had been dug out, and the total damage estimated, Shadbolt and Alington unanimously decided that the glamour and glory of war were definitely things of the past. Henceforth it was to be a matter of doing your duty to the limit of your nervous capacity, of suffering all things, not gladly but grimly, and of waiting patiently for the inevitable end. The light-hearted sense of adventure was over. The romance of war was dead.

EXTRACTS FROM LETTERS WRITTEN AT THE TIME

April 22nd, 1915. I managed to get a letter and a telegram off to you from the docks which I hope you received. We had the most perfect voyage over—smooth as a mill-pond and a clear, moonlight night. We were packed like sardines down below. Four of us subalterns shared a cigar box. We had to take turns as officer on watch. When my turn came from 12 to 1 a.m. I couldn't find my socks in the pitchy blackness. No lights were allowed, not even a match, I stumbled and fumbled about and woke everybody else up. I laughed till I cried. The others didn't. Then I went on the bridge with the Captain and watched the stars and the path the moon made on the water and felt wonderfully happy. It is a great thing to have your dearest wish gratified—especially after eight months' weary waiting.

April 26th, 1915. I don't know if you will be able to read this written on the march. My lorry is swaying like a beast in pain. I have sat on the front seat for two days now and am sick to death of the straight French roads with their trees on each side, the beautiful smiling countryside; and last, but not least, my air cushion, which has punctured! We have lost one officer already, Eric Leader, in the A. S. C. He was run over by a lorry the first day and broke his arm.

Later. We got in last night after dark. When I had put my men into barracks (very dirty French ones), got them some food and cleaned up the gun park, I set off down the road in search of dinner and bed. I couldn't find the first, except the inevitable bully, but I did find (oh joy!) a real bed and hot water to wash in. This town (Aire) is only 10 or 12 miles from the trenches, and we can hear the boom of the guns quite clearly.

May 4th. We have been in action the last two days and nights and I am very dirty and very busy still. I am longing for a decent sleep and wash. The first night, moving in, we didn't get any sleep at all, but last night I found an abandoned farm cart in our orchard. I jumped in, took my boots off and instantly dropped into a deep coma, which lasted till I was turned out by the sentry at dawn.

May 18th. Hotel de Lockharts, Chocolat Meunier Corner, France. The above is my address until further notice. It is our new observation post, a ruined house, bolstered up with sandbags. The whole place is really one massive sandbag with me in the middle. I am joined to the battery, a mile away, by a piece of telephone wire, and I look out all day on a vast expanse of nothing. At least that is what it looks like at first. It is really a piece of flat countryside corrugated with miles of trenches and teeming with human beings. Those wriggly, whitey-brown things are the trenches. You can't see the human beings. Yes, those two church spires and that factory chimney in the distance are real.

It is nice to hear you talk of flowers and sunshine. We have had nothing but drizzle here lately, and thick mud, like six inches of lukewarm butter, and ever since Saturday one continuous battle.

June 1st. The trenches here are most terribly complicated and confusing to a new-comer. They are much deeper and better built than those where we were before, and have evidently been dug a long time, for grass and even crops are sprouting from them. This is how to get to the O. P. by trench all the way. Straight up Regent Street, into Glasgow Road, turn to the right across Harley Street, and drop down Hertford Street. Where this trench forks at Marylebone Road, take the right hand turn to Willow Lane, then straight along or rather twist along, till you land in the telephonists' room in this ruined house. There are six of us in there, two officers and four men—all asleep except me and one wretched telephonist. It is frightfully hot and the fug is terrific. I must climb the ladder which leads to the upper chamber and have another look out, and a blow of fresh air.

June 9th. Still at the O. P. I think if those at home could see us now, we might forfeit a certain amount of sympathy. The horrors of war seem so remote. Jones and I are sitting in the hall of this fine house, being the coolest and most draughty place. Shirt sleeves and a handkerchief instead of collar and tie, are the order of the day. A table is between us on which is spread a very respectable luncheon including a bottle of wine. Books and magazines are strewn around. We sit back with our feet up. There is not a sound except the birds singing outside, and we are only a few hundred yards from the German front line. Life is very pleasant. It is always changing though. To-morrow the 'Pip-squeaks,' 'Woolly Bears,' 'Marias', and 'Johnsons' may be dropping into the poor old house, like tramps into a pub. To-day every one has gone to sleep in the sun.

July 12th. I would love to see *Push and Go* and Harry Tate. I want to get back for a bit now, just as much as I wanted to go out before. I long to go somewhere where I can't hear the shells coming or going. Except for a week in hospital, I've been over two months within easy field-gun range of the Hun, and one's nerves get a bit ragged I suppose. There is an 18-pounder just behind us, which goes through and through my ear drums every time it fires. We were shelled out of our last position and have since then been through all the discomfort of moving and settling in again.

I nearly got shot as a spy yesterday. A subaltern on the staff and myself, finding life at the O. P. overbearingly tedious, went out for a walk round the trenches. It appears that these had just been taken over by some Scottish Territorials. They saw us dodging about behind the houses and crouching in the long grass, so they decided to shoot on spec. Luckily they were stopped by an officer who came along and put us under arrest until we were able to explain. There's a lot of spy mania about.

July 18th. I have got a new job 24 hours on and 24 hours off observing from an enormous slag heap. You never saw such a place. It takes hours to climb to the top and there I sit, or rather huddle in a little sort of rabbit hutch, with the whole of Bocheland below me, in front, and the whole of France below me, behind. The most wonderful view. When Hans von Spitzbergen makes white and black puffs appear in a certain village below me, I talk down the telephone and similar puffs appear suddenly somewhere in Bocheland. There are some French gunners in an adjoining hutch. Have you ever heard an excited Frenchman talk down the telephone? It is a fearful and wonderful business. When I was relieved last night I would have scared a respectable coal-heaver. It had been windy all day, and I was black with coal dust from head to foot.

Later. There is nothing happening and the flies are astonishingly bad. At night they disappear, and the rats come out in hundreds. One of them ran across my face as I was dozing just before dawn. Why any self-respecting rat should trouble to climb to the top of this mountain of slag is a mystery. There can't be much food except what the telephonists throw away. I have been talking to a subaltern in another battery up here, who is just back from leave. We came to the conclusion that after the novelty had worn off, for sheer and unadulterated boredom, war could not be beaten. I also tried to analyse my feelings with regard to the Boche. I cannot feel any strong emotion about him. War from a gunner's point of view is much too impersonal for that. I regard him in the same sort of way as the person who lives at Wigan or at Southend. His ideas are totally alien to mine, and I do not want to live with him in the least. At the same time I do not want all this trouble of killing him. Is it entirely due to him that I live on a coal heap all day and suffer boredom and discomfort and occasional danger? I don't suppose it is. I mean the average Boche has got no more say in it than I have. It is the old gentlemen in brass hats on both sides, who are responsible.

CHAPTER 3

Winter, 1915-16—the Staff

It was at the end of July, 1915, a month after the events narrated in the last chapter, that Shadbolt received his telegram to report to the War Office about the sinking of the *Kenilworth*. Instead of being censured as he expected, for his share in the loss of a valuable cargo boat, he found himself posted to the staff of a newly-formed Division of Kitchener's Army, and, as A. D. C. to the Divisional Artillery Commander, within three days sailed for France once more.

As life on a small staff was much the same, whether the formation concerned dealt with field artillery or heavies, a short description of this particular headquarters will not be out of place here.

The staff organisation of the artillery in France consisted of the C. R. A. of the Division, a Brigadier-General who commanded the Divisional artillery, and the heavy artillery C. R. A. also a Brigadier-General, who commanded the heavy artillery of the corps. Each of these two C. R. A's was assisted by a Brigade-Major, who ran the tactical or fighting side of his command, and a Staff Captain who was responsible for the administrative side. In addition, from about the middle of 1916 onwards, the staff of the heavy artillery C. R. A. included a Counter-Battery Staff Officer, who, with a number of assistants, was responsible for the detection and neutralisation of all hostile batteries in the corps area.

The General Officer commanding all the artillery in the

Corps was known as the Corps C. R. A. He acted as technical artillery adviser to the Corps Commander, and issued orders dealing with artillery matters direct to the heavy artillery C. R. A., and the Divisional artillery C. R. A's. His rank was also that of Brigadier-General. His immediate superior was a Major General, who acted in the same capacity to the Army Commander at Army Headquarters. Finally there lived at G. H. Q. a General Officer, usually a Major-General, who as senior artillery officer in France, acted in the capacity of adviser in artillery matters to the Commander-in-Chief, and was responsible for all technical questions connected with the artillery in the theatre of war.

In August, 1915, the British Army took over from the French a good deal more of the line, and, for the first time since the Aisne, found itself once more in France. The Division, to which Shadbolt belonged, after a fortnight's Cook's tour in Flanders, detrained at Doullens and systematically took over from French troops that part of the line which lay about twelve miles to the west of that town.

Shadbolt's little party, after a more than usually unpleasant journey in a French train, packed in the trucks marked '40 *hommes, 10 chevaux'* which were as familiar a feature to the B. E. F. as the trenches themselves, arrived at the station at midnight. The General, Brigade-Major, and Staff Captain had motored on ahead. An 18-poun-der battery was also on the train, and there was a good deal of confusion in the darkness detraining horses and mules, wagons and guns and men.

No one came to meet the artillery headquarters staff. One of their wagons got hopelessly jammed between the platform and the truck, and Shadbolt, tired and irritable, began to curse impartially the absent Staff Captain, the incompetent staff sergeant-clerk in charge, the men under him, the wagon, the war, and everything and everybody else in sight. Suddenly there appeared out of the gloom a dapper little French officer. He was covered in medals, and positively beaming with *entente cordiale* and enthusiasm. Shaking hands warmly, he threw himself with Gallic exuberance into the business of shifting the recalcitrant wagon. Amid a flood of unintelligible advice from the Frenchman, this was eventually achieved. Overjoyed at this success, he shook hands warmly again. He then kept poor Shadbolt on the draughty platform another half hour describing in detail the geography of the town of Doullens, and the probable situation of Divisional Headquarters, passing from this subject without a break to the merits and demerits of the female population, pause for unfavourable comparison with that of his beloved Paris, reminding him that it was six months since he had last seen the Place de Vend6me, short history of his military career during this period, another pause for vivid description of cavalry charge led by himself against *'Us sales Boches'* in 1914, his opinion of habits and methods of warfare Of said animals, by contrast his opinion of brave Allies... but here Shadbolt managed to stem the torrent by showing evident signs of a desire for bed. Shaking hands warmly for the third time, and remembering, just in time, that the embrace on both cheeks was not the custom in the undemonstrative race to which *Monsieur le Capitaine* belonged, he disappeared into the darkness as suddenly as he had come.

The whole area was swarming with French troops. The next day and the next, they poured through the town in motor lorries, dusty, grimy and unshaven-looking ruffians singing 'Tipperary' and exchanging jokes with our men as they marched in.

The roads up to the front were crowded with batteries of 75's, all trailing southwards. The shaggy, ungroomed horses, the men slouching in their saddles, the harness tied together with string formed a marked contrast to the smart appearance of our artillery fresh from the 'spit and polish' of home service conditions.

This was one of the pet fads of the C. R. A., who could be very scathing about any lack of attention to the outer man amongst the troops under his command. Passing a young driver in the horse lines one day, whose chin, buttons, and boots were not all that they should have been, he sent for the Battery Commander, and inquired with biting sarcasm: 'Does this living dung-heap belong to you? Why don't you have him scraped up? He spoils the look of your horse lines.'

Our Allies, when battles were not in progress, believed in the principle of 'Live and let live' and one could not have chosen a more peaceful part of the front for the initiation of a new Division.

The General and his A. D. C. were riding home one evening after a tour of the trenches, when they got on to a curiously deserted bit of track. After trotting a short distance, Shadbolt chanced to glance over his shoulder, when he saw, to his horror, less than half a mile away the whole German trench system they had just been observing so carefully from the safety of a well-built O. P. There was nothing to be done but ride on. Heart in mouth, expecting every moment a salvo of whizz bangs or a spray of machine gun bullets, Shadbolt and the C. R. A., followed by their happily unconscious orderly, eventually cantered out of sight.

This peaceful state of affairs was soon altered when the British took over. Our Higher Command held the view that the enemy should never be left alone. Even when battles were not in progress, he was to be continually harassed by bombing raids, trench mortars, destructive shoots on selected points, and every form of trench warfare unpleasantness. This was called cultivating the offensive spirit, or alternatively 'the war of attrition.' Unfortunately, like the boomerang, it worked both ways, and the enemy, not unnaturally, became offensive too. To the humble trench dweller the French plan of fighting a definite battle or battles at the selected point or points and leaving the rest of the line in peace, seemed more sensible. There was nothing to be gained by killing ten Germans in a raid on Tuesday, and losing ten of our own men in the counter raid on Thursday. The process of attrition applied equally to the mind as well as the body, and this continual cultivation of the offensive spirit, instead of improving the morale was very liable to have exactly the opposite effect. On the other hand, absolutely fresh troops, with their offensive spirit unimpaired by cultivation, launched into a battle with the intention of obtaining a definite decisive result, seemed a more likely way to win the war. However, the trench dweller had no say in the winning of the war. He merely, in the end, won it. Before the Division actually took over the line and whilst the French troops were still handing over, the C. R. A. was sent home. He had distinguished himself at Mons and the Aisne as a Brigade Commander, and was full of enthusiasm for the New Army Divisional Artillery which he had trained from its formation. The Corps C. R. A., his immediate superior, had not been at Mons and was actually a year or two junior in regimental rank to the Divisional Brigadier. Both men were somewhat similar in character, with abundant confidence in their own opinions, and a tendency to detonate if those opinions were called in question. At their first meeting, General Box, of the Division, after enduring, with commendable self-control, a little well-meant patronage from General Cox, of the Corps, interrupted with the complaint that his guns were not supplied with the latest form of dial sight.

'My dear Box, in trench warfare the No. 7 dial sight is quite superfluous. You will find when you go into the line that your gun-layers will be able to shoot perfectly accurately with the No. 4 (or whatever it was!) with which you are issued. Of course I know it is some time since you were last out, and you probably did not see much actual fighting, but you will soon find your feet, and I am sure you will agree with me that No. 7's are quite unnecessary nowadays.'

Box, purple about the gills, and showing obvious signs of early eruption:

'I was at Mons, Le Cateau, the Marne and the Aisne, General Cox. I was also at Ypres in the battles of October 31st and November 11th. On the latter date my Brigade took on a battalion of the Prussian Guard practically single-handed, and I should like to tell you, sir, that if it hadn't been for the No.

7 dial sight, I should not be here to tell the tale. In fact I will go so far as to assert that the whole history of the part played by the British Army in 1914 would have been very different if the artillery had had to shoot with these prehistoric, utterly inaccurate, perfectly useless No. 4's.'

'Nonsense, General Box, the conditions of trench warfare are utterly different from those of 1914. I am afraid I cannot agree with you that the No. 4's are perfectly useless. Some very accurate shooting was carried out by my Division at Neuve Chapelle and Festubert, and they were fitted with No. 4's.'

'Well, sir, I must protest very strongly at being sent into the line inadequately armed. I do not consider that my Divisional Artillery are fit to go into action until they are issued with the No. 7 dial sight.'

The argument proceeded on these lines for a little longer, each protagonist becoming more emphatic and more absolutely certain that his own view was right. Finally they parted in an atmosphere of frigid politeness and mutual disapproval. Two days later a telegram arrived at Division from Army H. Q:

The Army Commander is of opinion that General Box's ideas are out-of-date, and that his services would be more valuable in the training of troops at home. He should be warned to proceed to England and report to War Office as soon as he has handed over to his successor, who will be appointed in the course of two or three days.

Poor Box was broken-hearted. His beloved Divisional Artillery, which he had been training for months, had not yet fired a round and he was sent home in disgrace. There was nothing to be done but to hand over to the tactfully sympathetic newcomer, General Bagshot, and go.

Unlike most stories of real life, and especially those of unstuck Generals, this one ends happily, for, after a month's reflective gardening, General Box was exhumed by an appreciative Home Command, and given another Divisional Artillery. This he took to France, and commanded with no little distinction on the Somme and at Messines, until he was eventually so badly wounded as to be unfit for further active service.

Shadbolt's new duties consisted of looking after the twenty horses and thirty odd men comprising the Headquarters Staff, running the officers' mess, and assisting the Staff Captain in the compilation of ammunition returns and office work generally. He was also supposed to assist the Brigade-Major with the collection and collation of intelligence, to be always at the beck and call of the General, and to make himself entirely responsible for the creature comforts and material welfare of all three. In addition, he was expected to act as French interpreter when circumstances required it. In other words the duties of an A. D. C. seemed to be a compendium of those of office boy, nursery-maid, and *maitre d'hotel,* a sort of Head-Bottle-Washer-in-Chief-and-in-Ordinary.

Shadbolt at first thought it would be very pleasant to wear red tabs and live apart from the daily stress of life in the line. He was fond of horses and looked forward to long rides in the back areas. He also expected to have his horizon widened, and to get a better perspective of the war as a whole as compared with the restricted view-point of the regimental officer. He soon discovered that this was not the case. The life of comparative security as a staff officer did not compensate for the loss of the comradeship of his equals, and the sense of sharing with the fighting man his dangers and discomforts, his joys and his griefs, his fear and misery and blessed relief, all those ever changing contrasts, which are, in fact, the innermost core of war.

Life on a small staff, like that of a Divisional artillery, was as domestic and restricted in outlook as that in a battery, with the added disadvantage of being more formal and monotonous. The presence of a General, however genial, must have a damping effect on the spirits of a young subaltern. His life can be compared to that of a junior clerk, living, dining, breakfasting, and lunching with the head of the firm. Besides, Generals, as a rule, are not genial. At least not in war-time. They are much too worried about whether they are going to lose their jobs, and what their immediate superiors are thinking about them. For in the Army the rhyme about the fleas was accurately exemplified. 'Great fleas have little fleas upon their backs to bite 'em, and little fleas have lesser fleas, and so *ad infinitum.*' Substituting Generals for fleas and greater for lesser, one can see this process going on right up to the Commander-in-Chief, who in turn is bitten by the Prime Minister or some big political flea at home.

Shadbolt met a lot of minor Generals during his six months' sojourn with the staff, and gained an insight into their lives and habits of thought, which stood him in good stead when he returned to regimental duty. He discovered, of course, that the popular conception of an autocratic old gentleman with a liver, who conducted his war on the principles inculcated in the Crimea, was quite wrong, as was also the no less erroneous impression that a General never went near the front line, but spent his time issuing orders based on second-hand information received in his luxuriously appointed chateau in rear.

Being an irreverent young officer, he soon divided his Generals into two classes. The sort who were always called 'Freddy' or 'Johnny' or 'Tom' by their contemporaries and superiors, and the sort who were not. The Freddys were gallant fellows, full of the old Army tradition, conservative to the core, and distrustful of all new-fangled methods, especially the promotion to high rank of civilian soldiers. They were not at all livery and bad-tempered, except when it suited them, but, on the contrary, usually excellent company, especially after dinner, full of reminiscences of the good old days, and how they played polo with Haig when they were subalterns together at Rumblebellypor in '85. When inspecting troops, they were all affability, provided their pet ideas had been given due prominence and attention. With one it might be clean corks in the men's water bottles, with another feet, with a third, gun platforms, and a fourth might have a passion for sanitation.

Whatever it was, so long as the inspected unit could produce it clean and in good order, nothing else mattered. The one subject on which it was quite certain no questions would ever be asked was 'Gunnery.' Freddy had long ago forgotten any gunnery he ever knew, and, in any case, was not going to give himself away by exposing his total ignorance of modern scientific methods. With horses it was a different matter. Here he was on safe ground. There was nothing he did not know about horses. But when it came to inspecting siege artillery, the wretched fellows had no horses, so he had to confine himself to the water bottles and the feet.

One of the most human and pleasant pastimes known to mankind is adverse criticism of one's elders and betters. It is so easy, and induces such a soothing glow of self-righteousness. One is filled with noble indignation that men so obviously incompetent should fill such high positions! No wonder that all men, from school-boyhood upwards, indulge in this pleasing and satisfying pursuit! Having just done so ourselves, and remembering how much malignant abuse has been written about Generals by civilians since the war, let us turn to the other side of the picture.

The other sort of Gunner General was the efficient type with brains. He was much quieter to meet than Freddy, and could usually be distinguished by the fact that he did not look like a General at all. Out of uniform he might have been a business man or a country gentleman, or even a politician. He worked eighteen hours a day, and he knew his 'job' inside out, wasting no time over frills. If this kind of General inspected a battery no amount of whitewash and 'spit and polish' could save an incompetent battery commander. When it was a question of complicated barrage tables, involving, perhaps, some hundred or more batteries, the General worked them out himself, and did not leave everything to his Brigade-Major. He and Fred shared only two things in common, their intolerance of the civilian intruder, and their loyalty to the old Army tradition.

Imagine a man who has spent all the best years of his life in a big commercial undertaking. Slowly he has worked his way up to be assistant-manager. Suddenly an unprecedented flood of business causes the undertaking to multiply itself indefinitely, and to extend its branches all over the world. Our assistant-manager is promoted, and all his friends become branch-managers as well. If he is careful and does well, there are still wonderful opportunities for further promotion. Would you be surprised if he regarded you, the clever interloper, with jealous suspicion or with scornful contempt, you, who knew nothing whatever about the business a year ago, and now hope shortly to be made a branch-manager yourself?

Another taunt was that Generals never came near the front line, except when things were quiet. This was grossly unfair. When a battle was in progress, obviously, their place was not in the front line. They were much too busy directing matters from headquarters, but in less strenuous times, a message that a battery was being heavily shelled, was the signal for Fred to hop into his car and hurry to the scene of action. His cheery and indomitable presence was often the first to put heart into the harassed and anxious battery commander.

The French were quite unable to understand why we had so many Generals. The man who held a position in the French Army corresponding to the C. R. A. of a Division or Brigadier-General commanding a Brigade, was a Colonel, so that they had four less Generals per Division than we had. And they did not cover them with red tabs and hats and arm-bands, so that they were not so conspicuous.

General Bagshot, to whom Shadbolt acted as A. D. C. after Box had gone, was averse to wearing red, and generally went about in a plain khaki hat and an old macintosh without any badges of rank. He did not expect to be saluted in this disguise, but he did strongly object if any officer failed to say good-morning to him. It is the custom of the Service for officers when they meet for the first time in the morning to greet each other with a good morning whether they are personally known to one another or not. A good many officers of the New Army were naturally ignorant of this. Should General Bagshot meet one and receive no reply to his good-morning, he would turn round in his car, and roar back at the unfortunate youth, 'Good-morning, damn you!' Then with a chuckle he would tell his chauffeur to drive on.

He had seen most of his service in India where, as a Major, he had gained some notoriety on the following counts;

1. unning a racing stable which was known all over India

2. dressing his whole battery in red shirts in defiance of the Inspector-General;

3. spending his spare time breaking up station clubs after dinner, assisted by his subalterns.

He used to boast that telegrams addressed to 'Bagshot, India' would always reach him, but no other hint of his former notoriety clung to his somewhat portly person. In appearance, he more closely resembled a broad-minded churchwarden than a Garibaldi with a penchant for smashing up social clubs. Nor, in spite of twenty years' service in India, was he at all the choleric General so often depicted in magazine stories. Whatever happened, even when dinner went wrong and the whisky ran out, General Bagshot remained unmoved and imperturbable. Shadbolt never once saw him lose his temper or even show irritation, however trying the circumstances. In spite of these good qualities, however, he never got any further than C. R. A. of his Division. He put it down himself to the fact that he was known to the Powers-That-Be as Brigadier-General Bagshot, and not as Johnnie or Bags.

One day a very big General indeed, a Freddy of the first magnitude from G. H. Q,. itself, announced his intention of coming to lunch.

'Give him plenty of port,' Bagshot said to Shadbolt, 'and if he calls me Bags, I shall get a Corps at least.'

The Great Man duly arrived, and, to the amusement of the staff, at the end of lunch, he did actually address his host as

'Bags, my boy.' But the effect must have Worn off very quickly, for poor old Bags remained Brigadier-General Bagshot, C. R. A. *n*th Division till the end of the war.

The Brigade-Major, a big fair man with a fiery blue eye, and a highly explosive temper, was not a popular man, and did not get on with Bags or the Staff Captain. The only person whom everybody did get on with was poor Shadbolt, who was too insignificant to count. This did not make for pleasant relations in the mess.

One day Shadbolt got permission to take the car to Amiens to do the Christmas shopping. The Brigade-Major, who was newly married, gave him careful instructions about chocolates which he wanted to send home to his wife. In the excitement of visiting once more a civilised town, Shadbolt forgot all about the chocolates until the shops were just closing. He was then only able to purchase a small 2 lb. bag instead of the large box he had been ordered to get. He presented these to the B. M. in the office next morning. The latter gave one look at the chocolates and then burst into a roar of rage. Picking up the offending bag he hurled it at the unhappy A. D. C. who fled, covered with chocolate, to the door, closing it just in time to avoid the office ink-pot which burst with a crash on the other side.

The Staff Captain was a rubber planter from Malay, with a rubber inside so far as whisky was concerned, and no regard whatever for old Army traditions, Brigade-Majors who threw ink-pots, nor the sacred caste of Generals. His day was spent unhappily dealing with the masses of correspondence which flooded the offices of every administrative branch. Everything from camouflage to cabbages, from gum boots to gun tarpaulins came within his jurisdiction.

He soon learnt how to play the Great Army Paper Game. It is called 'Passed to you, please' and consists in writing these magic words or alternatively 'For your Information and Necessary Action' on every memo or letter and sending it on to somebody else. This military indoor game is of great antiquity, and is believed to have been initiated by Julius Caesar during the second Gallic War as a means of keeping his staff employed, whilst he got on with the fighting. The advance of education has popularised the game, and it now forms an integral part of every properly organised military system.

The opening gambit usually starts from the very top or the very bottom. It is either up to Gunner Smith or the Quarter-Master-General to make the first move. Let us assume that Gunner Smith, in a moment of absent-mindedness, consumes his iron ration under the mistaken impression that by so doing he will stave off the pangs of hunger. The crime is duly discovered by the sergeant, or No. 1, of his section, who reports it to his section commander. The latter reports it to the B. C., who then writes to the Adjutant making a clean breast of the whole sordid story and asking for guidance as to how to obtain another iron ration. The Adjutant, an efficient young officer who knows his job, writes 'Forwarded' on it and sends it to the Staff Captain! It is then purely a matter of volleying up and on through all the grades and formations until the correspondence finally reaches the august eye of the Q. M. G. Anyone who writes more than 'Passed to you please' or 'forwarded' automatically wastes time and loses the respect of the other players by branding himself a novice. The Q. M. G. delivers judgment, and issues a three page memo of instructions as to the procedure to be adopted should such an unfortunate thing ever occur again. It is then passed back and the correct wording now is 'For your information and necessary action.' Finally, the pile of papers returns to the Battery Commander and can go no farther. Action has got to be taken. He sends for the quarter-master-sergeant and orders him to issue Gunner Smith with another iron ration out of store. The Q. M. S. then calls for his storeman and tells him to unpack that perishing case of tin rations and give one of them to that perishing perisher Gunner Smith. The net result is that, three months after the consumption of his original iron ration, Gunner Smith, should he still be alive, is provided with another, and everybody has enjoyed a very ably conducted rally of the Great Game in the interim.

The above is an illustration of a very simple case. It will be obvious to the meanest intelligence that the game is open to endless permutations and combinations, and that there are possibilities of introducing all sorts of subtleties whereby the unsuspecting player may be induced to take premature action, or to say more on paper than is absolutely necessary.

An amusing case occurred in a battery some time after this. An elderly bombardier was on duty at the O. P. when a shell burst on the parapet of the trench and buried him. He was dug out little the worse except for slight shock, but it was found that he had lost his set of false teeth. In spite of every effort to retrieve them the teeth failed to appear, and the loss was duly reported when the party returned to the battery. The Major, an absent-minded, but kindly soul, immediately indented for a new set and supported his claim by an ably-written and moving memo. A fortnight passed and nothing happened except that the bombardier grew visibly thinner. So the major wrote again an even more strongly worded note urging, in the interests of humanity, the immediate despatch of the teeth. The reply came in the form of a wire:

Dentures despatched on the 16th inst. A. A. A Please inform D. A. D. O. S. direct if not received A. A. A.

The major wrote to D.A.D.O.S. and another three weeks passed. By now the correspondence on this subject had grown into a thick pile, whilst the wretched bombardier was little more than the emaciated skeleton of his former self. Finally the Major had occasion to unlock the small tin dispatch box which contained all papers officially marked 'Secret and Confidential.' A small registered package caught his eye, which he had no recollection of ever having seen before. The missing teeth were then revealed to his astonished gaze. The Bombardier recovered, and the correspondence was eventually filed, but the mystery of how the teeth got into the box was never solved.

Another character, who must not be omitted from any description of the members of this headquarters staff, was the General's chauffeur, colloquially known as the Ginger Rabbit. This individual hailed from north of the Tweed, and owed his somewhat obvious nickname to the colour of his hair, and a method he had of nibbling food whilst awaiting the General's pleasure. Sitting hunched over his steering-wheel, placidly chewing the unexpired portion of the day's ration, while the General made a tour of the O. P.'s or visited some battery position, he perhaps more closely resembled a contemplative cow viewing life over the top bar of a gate. Beneath this bovine exterior, however, he concealed a sense of humour and the courage of a lion. He and Shadbolt became great friends. The Ginger Rabbit taught him how to drive the car and would sit imperturbably by his side, egging the novice on to fresh efforts, as they tore up the straight French roads at the maximum speed the old Sunbeam could attain. Finally Shadbolt bent the bonnet rather badly against a brick wall, and this practice, which was strictly against regulations, had to cease.

The day at headquarters was a long and tedious one. Shadbolt, if he was not wanted elsewhere, helped the Staff-Captain in the office, and in the evening, over the whisky bottle, listened to his uncensored tales of life in Malay. Dinner was a dreary meal. The General made his nightly joke about the food. As it was always the same joke, after a time it ceased to cause more than polite hilarity, swiftly quenched. The Brigade-Major glowered and smouldered, the Staff-Captain concentrated on the absorption of whisky, and the A. D. G. made brave efforts at conversation with each in turn. In fact life on a small headquarters was a dreary business altogether. Those in the gun lines, who jibed at the gilded staff, and envied them their life of comfort and immunity from shell fire, might have changed their tune had they tried it for a few months. Shadbolt endured it till early March, and then applied to rejoin the siege artillery.

Extracts From Letters Written At The Time

August 1st. There seem to be some good points about a staff officer's life. We landed on Saturday, and are now living in a large and sumptuous chateau about twenty miles from the line. I've got two horses to ride, one a beautiful black mare with perfect manners and a mouth like silk, and the other a wise old gentleman, who has obviously been a hunter before he took to soldiering. I have been appointed controller of the household and have to look after the material wants of 30 men, 20 horses, 4 officers, and a General. My chief trouble is the old hag of a *madame*, who has been left in charge here. I am the only one who can understand two words of French, and she gets so excited and talks so fast, it's generally only one word in six that I do understand. Everything is *defendu*, and it's always '*il n'iy a pas de ça*' when I want anything. Yesterday she was very upset because I turned the horses out into the paddock for a bite of grass. Ah! it was *defendu* and would I bring them in at once and pay for the grass they had already eaten. So I'm afraid I lost my temper a little, and told her it was *la guerre*, and that the sacred horses would therefore remain and eat her three times sacred grass. The local inhabitants are curiously unappreciative of a foreign occupation even though we are their brave allies.

Running the mess isn't as easy as I thought, especially as they all seem terribly particular about what they eat. Take tea, for instance. I go to endless trouble to provide butter and cake and jam, and the Brigade-Major complains because there's no shrimp paste!

November 7th. Have just returned from a four days' trip to Calais with the Old Man. We went to watch a wonderful hush-hush wire-cutting stunt on the sands. All the other Gunner Generals in the British Army came too. The first night I counted up to forty in the hotel —a fearful and wonderful sight. It occurred to me looking at some of them that it might be an advantage to die young after all.

Bags enjoyed himself immensely. He talked a lot of scandal

about those present, exceeded his normal ration of one whisky by one more, and regularly let himself go. The crowning touch was when a very big pot indeed called him Bags in front of several others. I met some old friends amongst the A. D. C.'s and compared notes. One day I shall write a book about Generals entitled *Brief Life History of the General in Peace and War,* with copious notes on the manners and habits of this now extinct fauna, price 30s., reduced to 1s. 6d. I suppose, after the war, they will be extinct. The successful ones will all be Field Marshals, or stockbrokers, the less efficient, and guinea-pig company directors.

November 11th. Madame says I am a *garçon de bonheur* born under a *belle etoile.* This because I sing in my bath. Well, I am very lucky to have a bath, but otherwise I don't see any cause for *bonheur.* If I don't get some leave soon I shall run 'amok' and stab the Divisional Commander with a bread knife. Life is exceedingly dull. I gather it's no more thrilling in the trenches. It's one of my jobs to compile the Intelligence Summary every day. All the little items of news from every O. P. on our front are sent into me. They are less exciting usually than the talk at an old lady's tea-party. This is the sort of thing. '10 a.m. All quiet. 11 a.m. A working party of four Germans was seen digging in S.5.b.25. 11.5 a.m. Working party dispersed. 1 p.m. Two bombs fell in our front trench about S.60.36. 4 p.m. All quiet. 10 p.m. German transport heard moving from the direction of the Berles-au-Bois.' Meanwhile it freezes and snows, and slushes alternately. Caesar's idea of going into winter quarters, and only waging war in the summer was a sound one.

My house-keeping worries are still with me. One of my chief troubles is the cook, a fat fellow, who is, I believe, a plumber in private life. The General described him last night as a greasy caterpillar, or alternatively, as a great fat, oily maggot. I must say he is not a good cook.

December 1st. You have my deepest sympathy, but at the same time, I can't help being amused at the cause of your complaint. There you are, the youngest subaltern in a battalion of Kitchener's Army, stationed only a few miles from London. On account of your O. T. G. experience and your well-known charm of manner, the Colonel has made you transport officer. So that already you have a command of your own, with the additional advantage of riding a horse, whilst everybody else walks. You have also got to know all the presentable girls in the district, beside several ravishing ones in the great and wicked Metropolis. All this is very bad for you, my lad. For what is the effect? Instead of enjoying your life of ease and amorous dalliance, you write and complain that the battalion has been ear-marked for home defence, and that you won't get out to France for months, and perhaps not at all. Fie! James. Why, I haven't seen a girl at all, let alone a pretty one, for six months. The only female I ever meet or talk to is old Madame Juillard, who lives in my billet. She remembers the Germans coming through the village in 1870, and her great delight is to get me into the kitchen for a gossip over a cup of coffee. She was interested to hear that I was 'fiancé.' The other night it was very cold, and the dear old girl insisted on producing a hot water bottle for me. I protested, as you know how I hate the smell of hot rubber. But Madame was firm. *'Quand il fait si froid, il faut que Monsieur le Capitaine couche avec sa fiancé,'* she said, popping the offending hot water bottle between the sheets.

She was much amused by the kilts of a Highland Regiment, which marched through the village this morning, and asked me if it is true *'qu'ils ne portent pas de caleçons au-dessous.'*

I am hoping to get leave before Christmas. I am longing to see some of the new shows, and to eat in a cheery restaurant again. Jane seems to go out every day of the week with cavalry, flying corps, sailors, Canadians, and even P. B. infantry like you. I tell her she is too indiscriminate, but she says she is doing her bit.

CHAPTER 4

The Somme—1916

When Shadbolt returned to siege artillery in March, 1916, he was posted to an 8 in. howitzer battery which was in action near the village of La Cauchie on the Somme front. This battery had been out since the end of 1915, but had so far seen no fighting and sustained no casualties. Shadbolt found considerable changes since the days of Festubert and Loos. The men were the same, with still the same magnificent standard of physique, no gunner stood under 6 ft., and every man was capable of lifting a 200 lb. shell single-handed, but the officers, with the exception of the Major and the Captain, were all New Army men. At first, he found it hard to get on with them, and to understand their point of view. They, on the other hand resented the sudden appearance of Shadbolt as senior subaltern. On principle, Regular officers were suspected of prejudice, especially those who had been on the staff.

The battery was armed with the early type of 8 in. howitzer. A makeshift piece of ordnance, it was manufactured by cutting off the muzzle of the 6 in. gun of the coast defence forts, reboring it, and mounting it on a special carriage with two huge wheels. Each wheel weighed a ton and stood as high as a man, and the whole contrivance weighed 14 tons. The method of traction was by caterpillar and the rate of travel about 12 miles per hour. The great shells, weighing 200 lb., were loaded by means of a crane fixed on the carriage itself. Two men brought up the shell on a special tray. It was then hoisted into position in

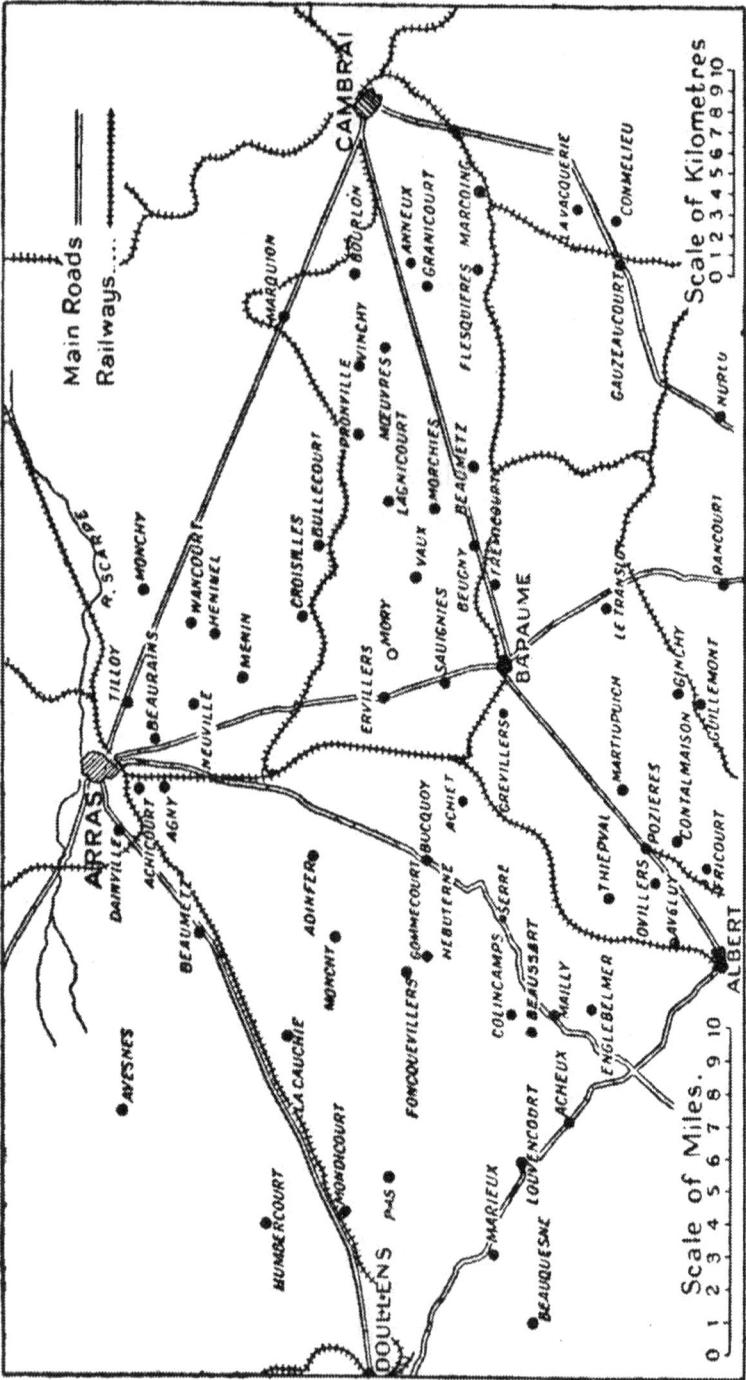

Main Roads ————
Railways ··········

CAMBRAI

Scale of Kilometres
0 1 2 3 4 5 6 7 8 9 10

LAVACQUERIE
CONNELIEU
BOURLON
ANNEUX
GRANICOURT
MARQUION
FLESQUIERES
MARCOING
GAUZEAUCOURT
NURLU
PRONVILLE
VINCHY
MŒUVRES
LAGNICOURT
VAUX
MORCHIES
BEAUMETZ
R. SCARPE
MONCHY
WANCOURT
HENINEL
CROISILLES
BULLECOURT
MENIN
TRESCOURT
BEUGNY
SAUGNIES
RANCOURT
TILLOY
BEAURAINS
NEUVILLE
ERVILLERS
OMORY
BAPAUME
LE TRANSLOY
GINCHY
ARRAS
DAINVILLE
ACHICOURT
AGNY
GREVILLERS
MARTINPUICH
POZIERES
CONTALMAISON
GUILLEMONT
BEAUMETZ
ADINFER
BUCQUOY
ACHIET
THIEPVAL
FRICOURT
MONCHT
GOMMECOURT
HEBUTERNE
SERRE
OVILLERS
AVGLUY
ALBERT
AVESNES
LA CAUCHIE
FONQUEVILLERS
COINCAMPS
BEAUSSART
MAILLY
ENGLEBELMER
ACHEUX
MARIEUX
MONCHOURT
PAS
LOUVENCOURT
HUMBERCOURT
BEAUQUESNE
DOULLENS

Scale of Miles.
0 1 2 3 4 5 6 7 8 9 10

front of the breech and two more men rammed it home with a heavy rammer. The cordite cartridge, weighing about 20 lb,, in a silk bag, was put in separately (as is the case with all howitzers). The breech was then closed, and a T-shaped brass tube containing gunpowder inserted in the vent hole at the base of the breech. A lanyard attached to this tube fired the gun. The maximum rate of fire was about one round a minute, and the maximum range was 10,000 yards (over 5½ miles).

The howitzer stood on a wooden platform, the recoil being taken by four enormous scotches, or wooden ramps, placed in front and behind the wheels. When the gun fired it ran up and down these ramps till it came to rest. The effect was that of some vast mastodon with its nose in the air painfully coughing out smoke and rolling back and forth with the effort.

The first of these heavy howitzers arrived in France about the middle of 1915. They were gradually replaced in 1916 and 1917 by a new and greatly improved pattern, weighing nearly 4 tons less, with modern methods of recuperation after recoil, and an increased range of 12,500 yards or over 7 miles; of these 246 were issued to the B. E. F. before the end of the war. A total expenditure of over four million rounds of 8 in. ammunition, equivalent to an average of two rounds a minute, was recorded between the outbreak of war and the Armistice.

In addition to a new type of officer and a new type of armament, Shadbolt was introduced to new and improved methods of shooting. Of these the most outstanding was shooting by aeroplane. Ranging by heavy and siege artillery by means of aeroplane observation was in its infancy in 1915, and Shadbolt had had no experience of it. The method eventually employed was a simple but effective one. The target was placed in the centre of an imaginary clock with 12 o'clock due north and 6 o'clock due south. Concentric circles were then drawn round the target at distances representing 25, 50, 100 and 200 yards. These circles were lettered A. B. C. and D. The aeroplane observer reported by wireless the fall of the rounds with reference to the circles, and the clock time. Thus

C.3. would be 100 yards from the target at 3 o'clock, in other words 100 yards due east. The clock code method, at it was called, had the double advantage of being simple to understand and of affording no information to the enemy.

Another great improvement was the system of issuing special large scale maps to the artillery on boards for convenience in handling. When a battery was ordered to a new position, the survey people were at once informed, and in consultation with the B. C., the exact location on the map of the pivot gun was accurately fixed by survey methods. A conspicuous feature on the landscape, such as a church spire or factory chimney was then selected and its position also fixed. This was known as the aiming point, and from it the angle between the gun and any given target could be measured. The map was then prepared showing our own trenches and those of the enemy and including all targets such as hostile batteries and enemy H. Q,. which had been definitely located by aerial photography or other means.

These maps were divided into squares, which were lettered and numbered in such a way that it was a simple matter to describe any point on the ground to within ten yards. As conditions did not always allow of observed fire, for instance at night, and on targets which were out of view from the ground, it was essential that artillery maps should be as detailed and accurate as possible.

Yet, given the most perfect map in the world, no gunner can be expected to drop a shell on the target at the first shot. This was a point which the infantry soldier never could understand. He would locate a concrete fortlet, or pill-box, concealing perhaps, a machine gun, which was worrying him, and ask the gunner to knock it out. He would chafe at the delay in opening fire, and end by complaining bitterly if the pill-box was still intact after half a dozen ranging rounds. One would hear subdued murmurs of 'Rotten shots these gunners. They couldn't hit a haystack once in a hundred times.'

Actually this remark was uncomfortably near the truth, but

it was not the fault of the gunners. It is a scientific fact that one hundred rounds fired all from the same gun, and at exactly the same range, under ideal conditions, may fall within an area 300 yards long by 40 yards wide. This area is known as the 100 per cent, zone, and varies for different ranges and for different natures of ordnance. Thus the 100 per cent, zone of a gun is usually larger than that of a howitzer, and the 100 per cent, zone of a 60-pounder firing at 10,000 yards is considerably larger than that of the same gun firing at 2,000 yards.

In addition to the 100 per cent, zone, the gunner has to compete with a large number of variable factors, all of which affect the shooting of the gun. Of these the most important are variations in ammunition, wear and tear of the gun itself, weather conditions, including temperature, wind, and barometric pressure, the temperature of the charge and map inaccuracies.

It will be easily understood from the above that of a hundred rounds fired at a haystack two miles away, only a small percentage might actually hit it. Alteration in weather conditions alone might make a difference of two or three hundred yards in the fall of a round between 8 a.m. and 10 a.m. In order to assist the artillery, meteorological stations were established along the front. These issued ' Meteor' telegrams every two hours giving the barometric pressure, the direction and force of the wind at different levels, and the air temperature at different heights.

The country was very different from that over which Shadbolt had fought at Festubert and Cuinchy. Instead of the flat, low-lying open country of Flanders, here was chalk hill and downland dotted with woods and copses, and with certain strongly marked features common to similar formations in England. Of these the most noticeable were the steep, regular banks or terraces, which the French call *remblais,* and our own country people lynchets, and the presence of roads or tracks sunk between two such banks forming a kind of narrow gully or ravine. It was in one of these tracks, its guns dug into the eastern bank, that the battery at La Cauchie was concealed.

The front line ran through Hebuterne, at the extreme northern end of what afterwards became the Somme battlefield. The Germans opposite occupied the Gommecourt salient, one of those projecting fortresses with which the enemy buttressed his front line. The enemy wire at this point was about four feet high and forty feet in depth, securely staked down with iron supports, and the distance between the opposing front line trenches not more than forty or fifty yards. In consequence there was much sniping from both sides.

The Major was up in the front line trench one day using a periscope with great care, as he had been warned about the activity of the enemy's snipers. He was accosted by an infantry private.

'I wouldn't put that up, sir, if I was you,' the man said.

'Why not?' replied the Major.

'Well, sir, I've had three of them peris knocked out this morning. I'm the Brigade Observer,' he added.

'Indeed,' said the gunner, 'well how do you observe?'

'Oh, I just puts my 'ead up,' was the reply.

The trenches, instead of being built up with sandbags, as in Flanders, were dug down into the chalk in some places from eight to twelve feet deep, their sides revetted, or held from collapsing, by wire netting. Dug-outs were cut in the sides of the trench, their roofs supported by curved pieces of iron, known as elephant iron. Our troops had not yet learned to dig deep dug-outs at the bottom of mine shafts, which we afterwards found (to our cost) throughout the whole of the enemy defence system.

All this part of the line was deathly quiet, but signs were not wanting that an attack on a large scale was pending. Behind the gun lines new roads were being cut and old ones re-metalled, vast dumps of ammunition were being accumulated, fresh divisions were being brought up, and every week new heavy and siege batteries arrived from England. Actually the number of heavy guns and howitzers in France was doubled between February and the end of June, 1916, the total number along the whole front on that date being 748. This compares with 276 during the battle of Loos, 100 at Festubert and 16 at Mons.

On the 1st May the first of the super-heavy guns arrived, three 9.2 in. and one 12 in. on railway mountings. Their ranges were about 15 and 19 miles respectively, and they were employed to shoot at railway junctions and towns behind the German lines, where headquarters of high formations and enemy reinforcements might be expected to concentrate.

Every effort was made to conceal these vast preparations from the enemy. Our aeroplanes were concentrated in large numbers behind the front, and air-fights provided a daily spectacle for the earth-bound pygmies below. By early June an enemy plane over our lines was a very rare sight. They had been temporarily driven out of the sky.

About this date the battery was ordered south, and after a night on the road came into action behind the village of Englebelmer. The howitzers were in an open field, the men and officers slept in tents and bivouacs in a little wood about a hundred yards to the flank. The allotment of ammunition for the preliminary bombardment was four to five hundred rounds per howitzer. Every night for a fortnight, hundreds of shells and cartridges were dumped in the battery position. The ammunition lorries were due to arrive as soon as darkness fell, but, owing to the congested state of the roads, they often did not appear till midnight or later. The cry of 'Ammunition up' brought sleepy men from their holes, lorry after lorry was unloaded, and the shells placed in heaps of twenty in the gun-pits or under cover in rear.

To get some idea of the labour involved, imagine that you have done a hard and continuous day's work, heavy work, digging gun-pits and dug-outs, lifting shells, and manoeuvring a 14-ton howitzer about a wooden platform. Sinking into a deep sleep, within an hour you are rudely wakened by the everlasting cry of 'Ammunition.' You stumble out to join the queue of grumbling men, and for the next two hours you carry 200 lb.

shells over rough ground in the dark. It was then that the fine physique of the garrison gunner stood him in good stead, and enabled him to endure this never-ending toil.

Behind the little encampment, on the extreme edge of the wood, lived Granny. Every time that Granny coughed, about once every three minutes when the battle began, the men resting from ammunition fatigues in their flimsy bivouacs, stirred fretfully in their sleep. For 'Granny' was a 15 in. howitzer, the largest of her kind in France. Two of her sisters lived in another small wood about two hundred yards in front of the battery.

These three super-heavy howitzers had landed in France in October, 1915. They were manned by the Marine Artillery, as actually they were naval weapons, loaned to the Army by the Admiralty. They fired a 1,500 lb. shell, and their maximum range was about 6 miles. To see one of Granny's shell land on a house in the enemy lines was an inspiring and awesome sight! There was a shattering explosion, followed by a thick column of reddish-black smoke rising as high as the dome of St. Paul's. Granny and her two sisters fired 1,400 rounds during the first week of the Somme battle. By the end of 1916 their number was increased to ten, but no more of these howitzers were landed in France after that date.

Alongside Granny's sisters a battery of 60-pounders added their staccato, ear-splitting bark to the deafening boom of the old ladies. In this small area about the size of the average country-house garden, lay concealed seven heavy howitzers and four heavy guns. In front of them and to their right and left were hundreds more, the greatest concentration of artillery ever known on any battlefield.

On June 20th the normal gun-fire was doubled along the whole front, and four days later was increased again until it reached the intensity of a full bombardment. The fire was continued throughout the night with the double object of leading the enemy to expect an attack at dawn and of preventing his supplies and reinforcements from reaching him. The next day no attack was made, but our aeroplanes raided the enemy observation balloons and destroyed nine of them.

All that day and night the bombardment went on, and the next day, and the day after that, but still no attack took place. To those in the gun-pits, the whole of life seemed to merge into one clanging, clashing, roar of sound. Covered with sweat and grime, the slaves of the gun toiled and laboured, ate, lay down and slept, and toiled and laboured again, to the roar and rush and scream of hundreds of hurrying shells. Their horizon was bounded by the vast and insatiable engine which they continuously fed. Their minds were numbed and deafened by the never-ceasing clamour of their gods.

From the O. P. Shadbolt looked out on the trenches round Serre, another enemy strong point, and saw the great shells spouting like waves on a lonely rock. The white chalk line of a piece of trench would appear through the billowing smoke, then a giant breaker would strike it, flinging up a cloud of black spray, then another, and another, and the whole would disappear again in writhing whirls of black and white smoke.

For seven summer days this tumult of Hell went on, and on the seventh hour of the seventh day gathered in force and volume so that the whole world seemed to rock with sound. Surely no human being could live under that terrible blasting and hammering! At half-past seven, some thousands of very gallant gentlemen, the flower of the English race, climbed over the parapet and started to walk the stretch of battered No Man's Land towards the German trenches. Instantly the air was filled with a new sound, the tearing rattle of enemy machine guns, and many of those brave men fell before they had taken a step. Others broke into a stumbling run, only to fall when less than half-way across. In front of Serre and Gommecourt the first day of the Somme battle was a bitter and tragic failure.

During the bombardment the Germans had taken refuge in their mined dug-outs, twenty feet under the ground, large enough in some cases to accommodate twenty or thirty men, and all with two or three shafts leading down into them, so that if one were blown in they could escape by another. Though suffering terribly from hunger, thirst and the continuous concussion, they were alive, and directly the bombardment lifted they ran up the steps of the shafts with their machine guns and mowed down our men like corn.

Meanwhile there was good news from the southern half of the battlefield, and the guns went pounding on. About 11 o'clock Shadbolt was in No. 4 gun-pit when a terrific explosion sent him spinning. One of the Grannies had blown up, killing all her crew and several wounded infantry, who were hobbling past. A shell had exploded prematurely in the bore, and lumps of red-hot metal were flung in every direction. A piece, the size of a football, fell at Shadbolt's feet.

As the day wore on, the intensity of the fire died down, and an ever-increasing number of walking wounded began to stream past the battery position. They spoke of failure and disaster, of the accurate and terrible enemy barrage on our trenches before the start, of the withering machine gun fire which met them as soon as they climbed over the parapet, of the snipers and machine guns hidden in holes and tunnels between the lines, who shot them in the back as soon as they had passed. They spoke of whole companies mown down as they stood, of dead men hung up on the uncut German wire like washing, of the wounded and dying lying out in No Man's Land in heaps.

So ended the 1st of July, a day which began with such high hopes, and ended, in this sector, at any rate, in bitter disappointment and death.

A week later the battery was ordered down to Albert. The Major and Captain went down to reconnoitre the new position, and Shadbolt was left in charge to pack up the stores and ammunition and pull out the guns. As soon as darkness fell, the work began. Each gun in turn, was man-handled out on to the road, hitched on to its caterpillar, and sent off to join the main body which was waiting, a mile or two away, out of range of enemy gun-fire. Towards midnight the last monster was being slowly heaved by two lines of men on ropes towards the waiting caterpillar when one wheel skidded. There was a lurch and a cry of dismay, and the big howitzer was axle deep in the ditch. Shadbolt called for more lanterns, put the whole of the battery available on the ropes, about fifty men on each, placed a 14-foot lever under the wheel and gave the order 'Heave.' The howitzer remained motionless. The caterpillar tractor was then brought up, very gingerly and not too near, for fear that it should sink in too. Another rope, about three inches thick, was tied to the tail of the caterpillar and the tail of the howitzer. All the men were removed except those on the lever and again the order given— 'Heave.' There was a resounding crack, and the caterpillar shot up the road. The howitzer stayed where it was.

The broken rope was doubled, the caterpillar brought back, and the men put back on the original ropes, care being taken that, should the doubled rope break, they were out of harm's way. Again the weary cry of 'Heave,' and the howitzer stirred very slightly, only to sink back again as soon as the strain was released.

Shadbolt was in despair. It wanted but an hour to dawn, when enemy aeroplanes might be expected. Should they spot the obstinate Behemoth, slumbering drunkenly in the ditch, life would become exceedingly unpleasant for all concerned. At this moment, help was forthcoming in the shape of an anxious A. S. G. officer, who had returned to find out what was happening to his fourth tractor. Grasping the situation at a glance, he promised to fetch two more caterpillars, and sped back along the road on his motorcycle.

A dawn, which gave promise of another lovely summer's day, was just breaking, when the promised help arrived. Feverishly hitching the three tractors in tandem on to the tail of the reluctant howitzer, Shadbolt gave one last shout of 'Heave.' There was a gurgling plop, and the cause of all the trouble rolled gently on to the road.

8-inch Howitzer in Difficulties on the Somme, 1916

The position in Albert was in a garden, a few hundred yards due north-east of the famous diving statue of the Virgin. From here the battery was able to shell Thiepval, Ovillers, Pozieres, Contalmaison and Mametz Wood, as each in turn became the objectives of our infantry. Observation posts were established, first on Usna Tara Hill, and later in Ovillers itself, and in the captured German trenches in front of Pozieres.

Little pictures of those days are flashed on the screen of memory. It is a brilliant summer day, fine and cloudless. The nearest German is two miles away. Shadbolt is sitting on top of the O. P. dug-out on the Usna Hill gazing through his glasses at the panorama of the Somme battlefield. In front of him, on the extreme left, can just be seen the tops of the trees of Aveluy Wood. Further to the right on the summit of that hill, lies a battered heap of brick-dust and chalk with a few skeleton trees flanking it—Thiepval. Further to the right still another similar heap—Ovillers. Straight in front, stark against the sky-line, is the broken village of Pozieres. The remains of a windmill shimmer in the heat haze just to the right, and, beyond it, one can plainly see the main road coming down the hill from the village and losing itself in a fold of the ground. It is the same road from Albert, which lies twenty yards away to his right and divides Usna Hill from Tara.

Two infantry officers have joined him and are sitting there discussing the length of life of a foot-soldier in France—a common topic. One, a middle-aged man, has been out twice already, and wounded twice. He does not expect a third reprieve. The other is more hopeful. He is young, and this is only his first time out. Both are talking bitterly about the man at home, who has never been out and never intends to come out. Shadbolt looks at the private in the Rifle Brigade, who is lying on his back in the grass about twenty yards away. He is not asleep. He was killed last night, walking up the road with his battalion.

Suddenly the puffs of white smoke bursting lazily over Pozieres cease to appear. A German ambulance, looking in the distance like a child's toy, winds its slow way down the road from the village. Shadbolt hands his glasses to the middle-aged man and asks him what he thinks of this strange phenomenon. 'Why it's a trick, of course. They are bringing down a supply of bombs and machine guns to the front line. Shoot at it, man, shoot for God's sake.'

But the gunner doesn't care to take the responsibility of being the only man on the front to open fire on the Red Cross. He contents himself with ringing up the battery and reporting it. Presently the ambulance disappears below the crest.

It is 4 o'clock of another summer's morning. Shadbolt is on the way to the O. P. He and two brawny gunners trudge silently past the large crater of La Boisselle, and the battery of 6 in. howitzers which is firing slowly and methodically towards the first faint fingers of the rising sun. The three are laden with telephones, reels of wire, gas masks, map boards, field glasses and food. Their eyes are heavy with want of sleep, their faces unshaven and lined with dust and grime. They turn up the empty road towards Ovillers. In front, the flame and tumult of the night's battle is slowly dying down, but a German 5- 9 in. is shelling the road where it breasts the top of the hill. Every thirty seconds exactly comes the droning whine of the approaching shell, followed by a deafening crash, and a column of brick-red smoke. Three figures appear walking, or rather stumbling towards them—a wounded Australian officer hobbling between two of his men. Shadbolt asks him if the battle has been a success. The officer doesn't bother to reply, but one of the Diggers says contemptuously, 'Our boys have captured all their objectives. I guess your people weren't in it.' Shadbolt, who has been up all night on the guns supporting the Australian attack, shrugs his shoulders and trudges on. He turns into the trench just below the top of the hill, passes the dead and swollen German, whose outstretched hand points the way to the O. P., jumps across the shell hole full of green and slimy water, and settles down with a sigh on the heap of sandbags and elephant iron which will constitute home for the next twenty-four hours.

A week or so later he is sitting in a captured trench near Contalmaison Wood. Pozieres, which is now in our hands, is going up in smoke and flame. All the morning he has been watching the tortured hill five hundred yards to the north. Great columns of earth and chalk and brick-dust are spouting into the air, and the smoke of the sacrifice swirls and eddies above them. 'The Major wants you on the telephone, sir.'

'Is that you, Shadbolt? The Colonel wants you to establish an O. P. in Pozieres. He thinks you will be able to see more from there.'

Shadbolt explains the situation. The Major is sorry, but orders are orders, and Shadbolt sets forth with a sinking heart. When he gets to the track at the bottom of the Pozieres hill, all signs of human life entirely vanish. Dead men and horses lie in heaps. A litter of smashed equipment and all the flotsam and jetsam of war obstruct his path. The hubbub of Hell is going on above, but here is an uncanny silence, the very valley of the shadow of death. He starts to climb the hill. As he gets into the edge of the barrage, an explosion seems to lift him bodily off the ground and blow him against a structure of sandbags and elephant iron. There are sounds of human voices, so he stumbles inside. Wiping the earth and mud from his eyes, Shadbolt sees that it is full of Diggers. They are all talking at the tops of their voices. He explains his errand, and is told that he must be quite mad. There is nobody alive in Pozieres except possibly a few men in the deep German dug-outs. There has been no news of them since dawn, as the telephone wires are all cut and no 'runner' can live in that storm of shelling. There are fifteen of them, the sole survivors of the whole company who went into the line last night. He points out that their sandbag structure is barely splinter-proof, and that any shell, like the one which knocked him down, could destroy the whole contraption. This seems to add to the general, high-pitched merriment. Shadbolt only waits for the suspicion of a lull outside, and then returns, faster than he came, to make his report to the Major.

Extracts From Letters Written At The Time

March 23rd. I haven't had exactly a rousing welcome to my new battery. True I have only met half of it so far, as the other half are in action about five miles away. The half I am with has been run, up to now, by the Captain and one subaltern. The Captain is a Regular, one of the dour, conscientious sort. He never smiles, at least I have never seen him do so. Once, about a week ago, I thought I saw his face kind of crack, but it closed up again almost immediately, and I may have been mistaken. I am certain he had never had a real laugh in his life. It seems dreadful to me, to take life and the war so seriously. If I didn't see the jokes in it I should find war quite unbearable. The subaltern, one Griffiths, is more human, but although I am relieving him of a load of work he seems rather to resent my appearance on the scene. Also, a most annoying trait, he has made up his mind that because I've come from the Staff, I know nothing whatever about guns or gunnery. He instructs in season and out of season. The Captain is inclined to be grandmotherly, too, so between the two of them, I'm nearly driven mad. The other day I was actually allowed on the guns by myself, whilst the other two went off to the mess for a meal. They hadn't been gone ten minutes before the telephone went. 'Don't forget to do so and so. Sergeant Smith will tell you what's wanted. Oh! by the way, have you remembered the such and such. Ask Sergeant Smith what to do.'

May 10th. We have joined forces with the rest of the battery and are probably moving down south. I like the Major immensely. He looks more like a scholar than a soldier, tall, with stooping shoulders and glasses, but he is full of laughter and talk, a human being. The Captain grimly, and with Spartan thoroughness, organises and orders, allots and arranges. Nothing, down to the minutest detail, is overlooked or forgotten. His gods are Duty, Discipline, System. The Major smiles benevolently, if somewhat vaguely, and only occasionally interferes. The other two subalterns seem to be quite good fellows.

One is a Scotsman from somewhere near Perth. His job is insurance, I think. He is also very earnest, but I think there is a vein of dry humour hidden
away in him somewhere. The other, whose name is Penrose, I know I am going to like. I cannot describe him to you, except that he is tall and big, and about my age. All I can say is that he is one of those people who gives you a feeling of friendship and understanding directly you meet him.

June 20th. We have been working so hard that I haven't had much time for writing. We are living under canvas in a little wood. I share a tent with Penrose, but the men are mostly in rough shelters and bivouacs, which they have made themselves by rigging up a mackintosh sheet over a hole in the ground. They have been working like navvies, digging and firing and moving ammunition all day, and then getting in more ammunition half the night. As usual they have been wonderful about it all. The other night I was listening to the battery humorist, a grey-haired old ruffian called Bennett. He was holding forth to a fatigue party about the horrors of war. He knew I was listening, which gave him an added zest. His remarks were quite unprintable, but the men were simply loving it and kept egging him on. To hear the British soldier really grousing at his cheerfullest and best, sounds to the uninitiated only one degree off open mutiny. Actually this is Tommy's way of keeping his spirits up, and of showing to others that he is still full of heart. I know, and the men know that I know, that they will work and fight till they drop, and that old Bennett will do the lion's share whilst he talks. If one night Bennett starts humping shell in complete silence and without one murmur of complaint, then I shall begin to be seriously worried.

July 8th. How shall I tell you about the battle! I've just been reading the papers, and they have got it all down much more clearly and vividly than I could ever hope to describe it. Also, they seemed to know a lot more about it than we did. Our knowledge is confined to what went on in our own little tiny sector. For the rest we depend on rumour. The preliminary bombardment was terrible. The noise was terrific and deafening. The air was filled with a rushing sound, as if invisible 'winged chariots and horsemen' were continuously passing overhead. The effect on the German trenches was like a storm at sea, a never-ending storm of spouting breakers against a defenceless coast.

CHAPTER 5

Arras—1917

At the end of August, 1916, Shadbolt was sent back from the Somme to assist in the training of the new batteries which were still being formed at home. By this date the heavy and siege batteries in France numbered about two hundred. All the Regular R. G. A. personnel had long since been absorbed, and there was a crying need in England for officers and N. C. O.'s with actual war experience to leaven the new batteries and to help in their training.

Shadbolt was posted to his old coast defence station at Tynemouth and was at once allotted 150 men, and told to make them into a battery. A Regular sergeant-major, who had been a young corporal-instructor in Gunnery in 1914, was told off to assist him. Unlike the sergeant-majors of fiction, he had the understanding and sympathy, which enabled him to deal in the right way with a collection of men who were unaccustomed to Army discipline. In addition, he possessed the unusual gift of being able to impart his own knowledge to others. He was, in fact, that *rara avis* among professional experts, an intelligent instructor. The men were from all ranks and conditions in life, farm labourers, shop assistants, factory hands, bank clerks, miners and office workers. None of them had ever seen a big gun, except perhaps on the pictures, but they were all keen and anxious to learn. The first thing to do was to sort them out according to their civil occupations. It was no good attempting to train as a telephonist the man who was a farm labourer or a navvy in civil life. The intelligent bank clerk was wasted as a mere heaver of shells. Men capable of being trained as specialists had to be carefully selected, and finally there were N. C. O.'s to be made and promoted as soon as made.

Within a week Shadbolt was ordered to take his army to Horsham, and the cheerful rabble, now denominated the 2XY Siege Battery R. G. A., entrained at Newcastle on the first of the journeys, which were eventually to land them as a fighting unit in France. At Horsham the organisation of the battery into a conglomerate whole, and the training of its several parts in their special duties went on apace. In addition to what may be called the combatant duties, men had to be found to act as cooks, officers' batmen, sanitary orderlies, and for other duties too numerous to mention. In France the bane of the B. S. M.'s life was keeping these duties within bounds. The men looked upon them as 'cushy' jobs, and when the work on the guns was heavy there was great competition for them. The following conversation overheard by a Brigade Medical Officer one morning in the line, illustrates their view-point. While waiting their turn for medical inspection the men on early morning 'sick parade' were lined up outside the Nissen hut, which had been allotted to the doctor. The walls of the hut were thin, and the M. O. making his preparations inside, overheard the following:

"Ullo, Bill, going sick again? Lot o' chaunce you've got with this mucking M. O. Why last week I was feeling queer so I tells 'im I've got the shivers all over, pain in the legs and feels sick. "Oh!" says 'e, so I goes on. "And I don't seem to want to eat," I says. "Oh!" says 'e. "Yes, sir," I says, "I don't seem to want to eat at all," I says. "Oh!" says 'e, "you can't eat your food?" Ah, now for light duty and a rest from 'eaving them blasted shells, I thinks. "No, sir," I says, "I'm afraid there's somethink wrong with my inside." "You don't seem to want to eat," 'e says. "No, sir, I don't," I says. "Well, *don't* eat," says 'e, the silly mucker!"

In October, Shadbolt was joined by Alington, home on sick leave and in the process of recovering from a complete breakdown after Loos. Shadbolt welcomed him with open arms, and took the opportunity to get married. After one day's honeymoon and that a Sunday, he returned to duty; for training a new battery in time of war meant in very truth 'to scorn delights and live laborious days.'

At last the battery was considered fit to shoot, and departed to Lydd to complete the last stage of its training. It was November, and conditions at Lydd had not changed for the better since that date two years earlier. The wind still howled over the desolate shingle flats. The rain and hail still beat the devil's tattoo on the roofs of the tin huts and iron gun-sheds. The whole place was packed with troops. Batteries were passing through at the rate of two or three a week. Shadbolt and his bride found shelter in a workman's cottage on the outskirts of the little village. The front door opened into the only living-room. Both of them had influenza, and Alington suffered from his usual heavy autumn cold, but no other officers had been posted and the work had to go on.

The next and last stage was at Codford, on Salisbury Plain. Here, at this time, the final mobilisation of a siege battery took place, before it was shipped to France. At Codford, the stores, guns and the mechanical transport were collected, the tin hats, gas respirators and field dressings were issued, and the last good-bye letters written. The only accommodation for married officers was in the village pub, to which Shadbolt repaired, after bidding a sad farewell to Legs' Eleven, who was pronounced by the doctors as still unfit for service overseas.

In addition to being the mobilisation centre for siege artillery, Codford was also a training ground for the Australians. Every night the rougher elements among these troops congregated in the bar of the 'George,' and an indescribable uproar as of wild beasts tearing each other limb from limb went on until closing time. Just before dawn the drafts for the front marched down the village street on their way to the station. In the darkness the sound of the *'Long, Long Trail,'* sung by several hundred male voices, would come nearer and nearer, swell to a full chorus beneath the bedroom window, and then gradually die away in the distance. One remembered that these men had come eleven thousand miles to fight for England, and that many would never return. For them the trail was indeed a long one, and a little 'relaxation' by the way was perhaps excusable.

The battery was due to sail at the end of December. A few days before Christmas several other officers were posted, and Shadbolt, feeling ill and tired, got leave to go home for three days. On Christmas Eve he developed mumps. A week later, the battery he had trained almost single-handed, the child he had brought up from birth, and for which he had slaved and toiled and sweated through four strenuous but happy months, sailed to France under another Battery Commander.

The close of the year 1916 brought the number of heavy guns and howitzers in France up to twelve hundred and fifty, five hundred more than there were at the beginning of the battle of the Somme. The year had seen the formation of seventy-six heavy batteries and one hundred and ninety-four siege batteries, two hundred and seventy new batteries in all. Of these, all but fifty were in action in France, the rest were either at home completing their training, or had been sent to other theatres of war. In 1915 only sixty-eight new batteries had been formed. The days of hasty improvisation were over. Woolwich and Lydd were now vast factories of war, working at high pressure, where men and guns went in at one end and batteries came out at the other. The penalty of unpreparedness was being wiped off. England was getting into her stride.

By the middle of January Shadbolt had completely recovered. Receiving no orders, he reported in person to the War Office. A harassed, but surprisingly amiable Brigadier-General greeted him with 'Where on earth have you been? I had completely lost you. I have been writing and wiring all over the country for you.' Somewhat flattered that so much importance was attached to his whereabouts, Shadbolt explained. 'Well, there's a battery at Codford, I forget the number, due to sail for France on Sunday. The O. C. has gone sick. You are to take command. You had better go down to Codford at once and report to the Camp Commandant. Your rank from to-day is Acting-Captain.'

He had four days in which to take over his new battery, collect his kit, and say good-bye to his wife. The officer who handed over 2XX siege battery, was cheerful but unhelpful. It appeared that his complaint was pyorrhea, and he was more interested in the impending removal of his teeth than in the departure of the battery. The state of the unit which he passed on to his unfortunate successor was also no concern of his, nor apparently had it ever been, judging by the condition in which Shadbolt found the battery, when he had time to look round. This officer was a keen poker player, and had a fund of amusing but unprintable stories which would have made him a success in any bar. These and a fondness for the company of the opposite sex, preferably of inferior social station, consti-tuted his only hobbies. In soldiering as soldiering, he took no interest whatsoever. He offered his successor the hospitality of his room for the night, told him the best of his stories, and departed in the morning full of gin and geniality, but without having handed over one trouser button.

Shadbolt went out to have a look at the battery drawn up on parade with its four new 6 in. howitzers. He was greeted by a grave elderly subaltern whose name turned out to be Tyler. Another very small one, also rather elderly, fidgeted about in rear. He asked where the third subaltern was. 'Oh, Lewis, sir, I expect he's in bed still. He never turns up before eleven.' The small subaltern was introduced as Macindoe. It appeared that he came from somewhere in the north of Scotland and was a professor of Theosophy, whatever that might be. Shad-bolt was not quite sure, but it did not sound a very hopeful in-troduction to the science of gunnery. At this moment Master Lewis appeared, a cheerful young oaf of about twenty-one, looking rather bleary about the eye, but full of self-confidence and brotherly love. He saluted perfunctorily and asked Shadbolt if he had slept well. Shadbolt returned the compliment. The men seemed to be a fine, upstanding, husky-looking lot. Shadbolt noticed one rather beery-looking sergeant, of the type known as 'Old Sweat.' He and the sergeant-major were the only two who had seen service in France.

Later in the day another subaltern reported for duty. He was a man of about Shadbolt's age, twenty-four, with a red, jolly face and an air of practical efficiency which at once put heart into the now thoroughly depressed B. C. John Hickling had started the war as a corporal in an early siege battery, in which he had gained the D.C.M. and a commission. He was the type of ranker officer to whom the British Army owes so much, capable, reliable, unimaginative, a rock-like figure amongst that crowd of semi-trained, ill-disciplined, but enthusiastic novices.

For there was no getting away from the fact that 2XX siege battery was semi-trained and ill-disciplined, and quite unfit for active service. In order to cope with the demand from the Front, batteries were being rushed through their training at home at such a rate that occasionally they escaped the vigilance of the experts at Lydd, whose duty it was to report on their fitness for war after they had completed their shooting on the ranges.

On a Sunday in late January, Shadbolt, with a sinking heart, set sail for France for the third time with a new and untried unit. The weather was bitterly cold, snow was lying on the ground, and the week spent under canvas in a base camp at Havre was not a cheerful beginning. That important person, the battery quartermaster-sergeant turned out to be thoroughly incompetent, and was short of everything. He was short of blankets, short of dixies in which to cook hot food, short of overcoats, short of gun stores, and short of breath. Fat and wheezy, a growth of dirty stubble on his chin, he came groaning into the tent, which constituted the battery office, to tell Shadbolt the story of all the contractors and ordnance store-men at Codford, who had done him out of his just dues.

Shadbolt contemplated throwing the ink-pot at him, but as the ink was frozen solid inside decided it would be safer and more dignified not to. He regretted this self-restraint a week later when the battery went into the line at Dainville, near Arras, and the Q. M. S. appeared again, breathing heavily, still short of blankets, dixies, coal, rations, elephant iron, pit props for dug-outs, camouflage and everything else essential for the comfort, well-being and safety of a self-respecting unit in the line. He had been told where and how to get these necessities of life and had been sent off with two lorries to get them. Needless to say he returned with a long story of all the difficulties encountered, but no stores.

The duty of the B. Q. M. S. was to obtain for his battery, by hook or by crook, by fair means or foul, a surplus of all those stores, including rations and clothing, which were necessary to its existence. The perfect Q. M. S. possessed a poker face, a silver tongue, an iron head and no moral sense whatever. If he could not get what he wanted by regular means there was an Army verb to 'scrounge' which covered all the methods employed by the most distinguished members of the criminal profession. In fact, it is probable that most of the successful crooks of Europe since the war are retired Q. M. S's from the armies. The Q. M. S. allotted to 2XX brought shame on this fine body of dishonourable men, and was quickly removed to a less important position. His successor proved a master of his craft, and remained with the battery till the end of the war, never failing to provide bread, when everybody else had biscuits, rum when there was no rum to be had, pit props when pit props were unobtainable, and all the other necessities and luxuries so essential to the maintenance of the fighting spirit. An example of his quality is shown by the following incident which occurred early in 1918. The battery was short of a number of expensive but useless stores, which had been lost during the travels and battles of the previous year. Among other things a blacksmith's forge, laid down in Army Form G 1098 as part of the equipment of a siege battery, was missing. On a certain Monday evening a battery of 6 in. guns, fresh from England, joined the Brigade to which 2XX belonged, and during the night came into action about a quarter of a mile in rear. At mid-day on Tuesday the Q. M. S. reported to Shadbolt that he had been able to obtain possession of an unwanted forge. Knowing his Q. M. S. Shadbolt did not probe too deeply into this somewhat ingenuous explanation of how a brand new forge had suddenly appeared amongst the stores. Four months later, he shared a cabin on the leave boat with the B. C. of the 6 in. guns and was told the piteous story of how he had been robbed of a forge, the moment he had set foot in France! His suspicions as to his Q. M. S.'s source of supply were thus definitely confirmed, but under the circumstances an assumption of complete innocence, combined with a tactfully expressed sympathy, seemed the only possible attitude to adopt.

Those first six weeks in the line were a nightmare to Shadbolt. In addition to all the ordinary work connected with running a battery in action, such as the selection of observation posts, the laying out of the telephone system, the registration of targets, the building of dugouts and shelters, and the organisation of reliefs and fatigues, this battery had to be trained. Furthermore, this all too obvious fact had to be concealed from the extremely vigilant eye of the Corps heavy artillery Commander, Brigadier-General K. K. Keiller, C. M. G. Had the utter unfitness of 2XX for service in the field been discovered by K. K. K. no explanation would have saved the B. C. from a return to subaltern's rank and an ignominious departure from the scene of action. Unfortunately the Colonel of the group of batteries to which 2XX was affiliated was not the kind of man to help a young B. C. in a difficulty of this sort. Tall and broad-chested, with slightly protuberant eyes, flowing moustaches, and a stately manner, Colonel Witchall looked every inch a soldier. Unfortunately his ideas on soldiering coincided with his appearance. He was the old-fashioned kind of army officer to whom clean buttons and a smart salute were the outward and visible signs of an inward and spiritual military grace. His only experience of work with the guns had been with a fully trained regular heavy battery in the early days of the war, and he had no sympathy with civilians struggling to learn a new trade, nor any understanding of their difficulties. He would take no responsibility which might damage his own prospects or shake his somewhat precarious hold on his position as Commander of a heavy artillery group. Fortunately, in outward appearance the men of 2XX were clean and not unsoldierly, and it was therefore an easy matter, when the Colonel paid a visit, to conceal those shortcomings and deficiencies which would have been immediately apparent to a more knowledgeable inspecting officer.

K. K. K. was a very different type of soldier, A mountain gunner who had seen service on the frontier, he was brave as a lion, hard as nails, knew his job and got on with it. On his very first visit he discovered within five minutes, the shortage of dixies and coal, the lack of elephant iron and pit props for dug-outs, and a number of other things Shadbolt would gladly have kept hidden. He started asking questions. 'I suppose Colonel Witchall, that this battery has shot in on its datum point? What observation posts are they using? Can they reach the German reserve lines in Monchy from here?' The Colonel sucked his straggling moustache and goggled appealingly at the B. C. Shadbolt supplied the necessary answers. The General turned to him. 'Now, Major Shadbolt' (Shadbolt was now Acting-Major and Hick-ling Acting-Captain) 'I want you to show me where your men sleep at night. The actual gun detachments, of course, sleep on the guns, but where are the dug-outs for the rest of the battery?'

The detachments did not sleep on the guns, but Shadbolt had a sudden intuition that this was one of the special fads of this unpleasantly efficient general. So he assured him that they did, and began showing him round the position, steering him as far away as possible from the spot about fifteen yards in rear and to the flank of the line of guns, where Hickling was superintending the digging of dug-outs for the detachments.

However, K. K. K. was not the sort of man to be steered by anybody, and he presently fetched up in front of Hickling.

'Good morning, Captain Hickling. I think we have met before sometime.'

'Yes, sir, in 1915'.

'Where do your gun detachments sleep?' Hickling remembered other things besides meeting the General in 1915.

'On the guns, sir.'

'What are you building there?'

'Dug-outs for ammunition, sir.'

'Ah, very good, very good. Show me your B. C. post, Major Shadbolt. I should like to see the zone of fire of your battery on the artillery board.'

For a month, either Shadbolt or Hickling lived permanently in the gun position. Not a round was fired by night or day without one of them first checking the calculations and the actual laying of each gun. If an observed shoot from the ground was in the programme, one would join the subaltern in the O. P. and conduct the shoot, whilst the other remained in the battery and saw that no mistakes were made from that end.

Among the subalterns Thomas Tyler alone was reliable and helpful. He was old enough to be Shadbolt's father and before the war, had achieved a name for himself as a writer. A great lover of the countryside, and of all God's clean and pleasant things it must have been special hell for him to live and fight in the mud and foulness and never-ceasing din of war, his only relaxation at night the battery gramophone grinding out fox-trots and the barrack room jokes of Hickling and Lewis.

He carried on quietly and patiently until he was killed about two months later. His serene and kindly presence and quiet, dry humour did much to alleviate the squalid miseries of life for his companions. Little Macindoe turned out to be even more theosophical than his grotesque appearance would lead one to expect. His anxious little face peered out from under his tin helmet with an air of pathetic bewilderment at this strange new world in which he found himself, and to the end, he was never able to grasp the mysteries of laying out the line of fire, or the rudiments of looking after his section. On the first day in the line, gun-drill was in progress, and Macindoe was in charge. After piping out various orders in his high falsetto, he was suddenly heard to scream 'Shut that door, please' to the men on the nearest gun. The puzzled gunners looked at the No. 1 who in turn gazed enquiringly at little Mac. 'Shut that door, can't you hear me?' repeated the anxious little voice. At that moment light dawned on a quick-witted gunner, and he closed the open breech with a clang.

Shadbolt took him up to the O. P., a sandbagged house on the outskirts of the town of Arras. Hung round with map cases, field glasses, revolver, gas mask, compasses and every conceivable gadget, his tin hat several sizes too large for him, and his little thin legs trotting eagerly beside his companion, the professor looked more like a clown at a circus than a gunner officer entrusted for the day with the shooting of four of the most modern engines of destruction. Their walk led them through a heavily bombarded portion of the town. Every few hundred yards, little Mac would stop, remove his helmet, and gaze wonderingly at the havoc and ruin around him. His companion would break into his philosophical dissertation on the horrors of war by gently reminding him that there were more hygienic neighbourhoods for the airing of intellectual thought, and that a German 5.9 might at any moment make the horrors of war most unpleasantly realistic. On arriving at the O. P. he scrambled eagerly up the ladder to the upper room from which observation was carried out. Forgetting this time even to remove his tin hat, he gazed entranced at the scene of desolation which represented the acme of achievement of two civilised nations at war. Shadbolt endeavoured to trace out for him the various features of the country from the map, and to point out the different targets on which he might be expected to shoot. All in vain! The professor was in another world, a world perhaps where the gods of mythology battled with thunderbolts and chariots of fire, where Zeus came down from Olympus and slew battalions with his breath: a world to which Shadbolt was certainly too earthbound to follow him.

At the end of the month he regretfully reported Macindoe as unfitted for service in the field. Regretfully because, although the professor was quite useless, he was lovable in his eccentricities, and desperately anxious to do his best. He was returned to England and eventually removed from the army.

Lewis, the third subaltern, was of a different type. The only son of rich and doting parents, he had been brought up to have his every whim gratified. A good lad at heart, the words 'discipline' and 'duty' had no meaning for him. He had never in his life been compelled to do anything that he disliked doing. When he joined the army he was under the mistaken impression that this Utopian state of affairs would continue, and had been confirmed in this impression by his previous B. C. Shadbolt found him very difficult to deal with as, unless he actually saw him carry out his orders, he could never be quite sure that they would be obeyed.

The reactions to the military system or to what has been called 'militarism' were many and varied. On senior officers like Colonel Witchall, whose lives had been guided by its tenets since boyhood, it produced a complete rigidity of outlook, as if their minds had been set in plaster of Paris at some early date and had been moulded in that fixed framework ever since. All men in uniform must conform to their conception of soldiers. The conduct of all wars must accord with the teachings laid down in the manuals, and the precedents established by the historical records of the past. Without exercise the muscles of the body stiffen and eventually atrophy, and this applies equally to the mind. Colonel Witchall, and there were many like him, was quite unable to grasp the changed conditions into which whole nations at war had thrown the military machine. The shibboleths and conventions of the little community in which he had spent his life, had been cast down and utterly destroyed. Initiative, enterprise and an understanding of human nature were the only passwords to success in this vast conflict for international supremacy, and personal selfishness wrapped in hidebound tradition must be sacrificed on the altar of the past, if battalions and brigades, regiments and armies, were to be led to victory.

At the other end of the scale the effect of militarism on boys like Lewis was equally deplorable. Unaccustomed to any form of discipline, they regarded all rules, regulations and orders as the instruments of a pointless tyranny, to be evaded if possible, to be perfunctorily carried out if obedience was unavoidable. To men like Macindoe these military rules and shibboleths seemed so stern and uncompromising that, in the effort to alter their whole outlook on life, the limit of elasticity was reached and they broke. Both types failed to understand that military discipline was originally invented as an aid to the soldier, and that to those accustomed to its workings it was not a taskmaster nor a tyrant, but an unconscious support in times of difficulty and danger. In the same way, military tradition, which has been built up through discipline, enabled whole battalions and batteries, as well as the individual, to face annihilation undaunted, and, countless times in the annals of our history, to emerge victorious from what seemed certain defeat.

Early in March, 2XX began to take shape as an effective fighting unit. It was no longer necessary to post a look-out to give warning "of the approach of K. K. K. The B. C. could leave the gun position for a few hours without speculating on his return as to what special calamity had befallen during his absence. It was about this time that the enemy made a strategic retirement in front of Arras, to take up a more strongly defensive line several miles further east. Rumours of a big offensive in the spring had been circulating and unmistakable signs were not wanting of preparations for a bombardment on a colossal scale, but this unexpected move of the Germans upset all the British plans. Whilst new ones were being made by the General Staff, the troops in the line moved forward to conform with the enemy retirement.

The new position selected for the battery was in a disused quarry pit a few hundred yards south of the village of Achicourt. From now on the preparations for the great offensive were ceaselessly pushed forward. Shadbolt was reminded of the time before the Somme battle, nine months earlier, with this difference, that now the number of guns seemed double as great, and the piles of ammunition that were dumped nightly on the battery positions, twice as many. A few hundred yards across the plain in front of the quarry lay a sunken road, which ran parallel to the enemy front. This road had to be crossed on the way to the O. P. At the end of February there were two field batteries in it. By the middle of March it was lined with guns and howitzers standing almost literally wheel to wheel, and as far as the eye could reach. The weather, by contrast to the warm summer days of the Somme preparation, was wild and wintry, with showers of sleet and hail. Roads and tracks, trenches and battery positions, were soon churned up into thick mud by the increased traffic. This made the ammunition and other fatigues doubly heavy.

On March 25th the preliminary bombardment began and continued without cessation until the 8th of April. During this period over 2J million rounds were expended at a cost to the taxpayer of thirteen million pounds sterling. On the last day the General Staff organised a full dress rehearsal of the barrage for the morrow and at the same time the enemy began a heavy bombardment of Achicourt and the surrounding area. An ammunition column, which, for some unexplained reason, was driving through the main street in daylight, was caught, and the blazing exploding lorries turned what had once been a thriving country village, into a holocaust of flame and death.

The quarry was about thirty yards wide by a hundred long. In order to enable them to clear the lip of the forward bank, the guns were placed with their trails against the backward slope where they were quite exposed, without gun pits or shelter of any kind. Shells were raining into the position when the time for firing the practice barrage arrived, but by one of those inexplicable turns of fortune, no casualties were sustained. A 5.9 plunged into the ground a foot from Tyler, and failed to explode though the wind of its passing knocked him down. That night in the mess somebody said, 'Thomas, you were evidently born to live through this war,' and they all drank his health. At 7 o'clock the next morning he was killed in the O. P. by a direct hit through the chest.

Easter Sunday, April 9th, dawned cold and wintry. Heavy black clouds in the eastern sky portended snow and bad weather. They hung like a menace of evil over the promised land, on which the shells were bursting with a slow and languid monotony, as if weary of this endless business of destruction. In the packed trenches, long lines of haggard-faced men, bayonets fixed and gas masks at the alert, waited impatiently for the zero hour. In the gun positions, shells were being fused and final preparations made to launch that storm of metal, which, like a solid wall of flying death, should move before our infantry, from trench to trench, from stronghold to stronghold.

Shadbolt looked at his watch. It wanted two minutes to the hour. Tyler should be at the O. P. by now. He had started late. That 9-2 battery behind were ramming their shells home badly.[1] Why was the fool firing at all. Nobody else was. Behindhand with his night's allotment most likely, incompetent ass! Why didn't Tyler ring up? CRASH! The air was rent with a swelling thunder of sound, stunning, ear-splitting, deafening. The Battle of Arras had begun.

A few minutes later a telephone message from the O. P. brought the sad news of Tyler's death. Soon after breakfast it was reported that all objectives had been taken and by mid-day the battery was ordered to cease fire. The enemy was out of range.

That afternoon it began to snow. About 4 o'clock, large bodies of cavalry passed up the road towards the front. Shadbolt's conception of cavalry was derived from stories of Wa-

---

1. Shells that were not properly rammed home in the bore, left the muzzle with a peculiar whistling ululation that was quite unmistakable.

8-inch Howitzer Position near Blangy, Battle of Arras, 1917

terloo and Balaclava, and from pre-war reviews on the Curragh or at Aldershot. In his mind's eye, Lancers, Hussars, and Dragoons swept by with fluttering pennons, tossing plumes and flowing manes. The sun shone on lance tip and sword blade, on breast-plates and gold braid. The air was filled with the glitter and jingle of steel, and the roll of the galloping hoofs. But here were men like his own gunners, only not so big, trotting past on hairy-looking little horses, muddied to their hocks. They were hung round with gas masks, waterbottles, haversacks and rifles, and their horses with feed bags, swords, greatcoats, blankets and more feed bags. It did not seem possible that they could ever move faster than a trot. The snow fell on their hunched shoulders and dripping capes. Did Napoleon's cavalry advance on Moscow like this? Some gunners raised a feeble cheer. But for him, one more romance of war was dead. He turned disconsolately away.

For three days there was nothing to do but clean up and listen to rumours. The body of poor Tyler was brought down from the O. P. and buried with all the honours of war. The honours of war! To be sewn up in a blanket and laid in a hole in the ground, a few hurried words muttered over the grave by an overworked chaplain, a sigh and perhaps a prayer from the friend standing by, then the hole filled up and that is all. Shadbolt remembered those lines of Rupert Brooke: "If I should die, think only this of me: That there's some corner of a foreign field that is for ever England," and was comforted.

He went forward with the Colonel and other Battery Commanders in the Group, to reconnoitre for new positions, and on the fourth day the battery was ordered to move. The country, over which the advance was made, was open rolling downland much like Salisbury Plain, with but one narrow road leading towards the front. Once the late battle area had been passed, it was an easy matter for all but the heavier natures of ordnance to move forward across the open. To avoid the congestion on the road it was therefore decided to put girdles on the 6 in. howitzers, and to tow them over the downs with four borrowed caterpillars. The girdles were wooden contraptions fixed round the wheels of the howitzers to prevent them from sinking in heavy ground. They were also used as a substitute for platforms when it was necessary to come into action quickly in a new position.

The places of Macindoe and Tyler had been filled by two new subalterns. One of them, aged about twenty-five, whose name was Davies, seemed a level-headed and sensible fellow. The other, Rawson, was a boy straight from school.

It was dark before the order to advance was received. For some reason, the caterpillars were late in arriving, and when they did come they got boxed up in the narrow entrance to the quarry with the lorries, which were there to collect the ammunition and stores. Finally, amid much shouting and blasphemy, the caterpillars and guns with their crews drew clear, and it was after midnight, when, with Davies, the new subaltern in charge, they started on their five mile trek to the line.

Shadbolt had some misgivings about sending poor Davies alone with this menagerie, to travel in the darkness across an unknown country to a destination marked by flags stuck in the middle of an open down. Unfortunately it was unavoidable. Hickling, for some reason, was away. Somebody responsible had to stay behind and see that the multitude of stores and the ammunition were packed in the lorries, and that this second convoy was also started safely on its way. Shadbolt then hoped to catch up the slow-moving caterpillars and bring the guns into action himself. The Colonel had been most emphatic that the battery should be in action by dawn.

An hour before dawn the last lorry left the quarry. Leaving the convoy in charge of Lewis, with accurate directions as to the route to be taken, Shadbolt hurried on to catch up the guns. As dawn was breaking he arrived at the appointed battery position. Not a soul was in sight. Save for a lark winging its way towards the empyrean, the whole countryside was entirely devoid of life. Presently a solitary aeroplane appeared, droning leisurely westward. He scanned it anxiously lest it should be a Fokker. Reassured, he turned his gaze once more earthwards to watch an 18-pounder battery come trotting forward over the crest towards him. As the guns and horses drew nearer he recognised that it belonged to his old division of the days before the Somme. Chains jingling, guns and limbers bumping, they looked a pretty sight in the early sunshine as they moved forward in close column over the grass. The B. C. at their head, on a nice-looking chestnut mare, gave him a cheery 'View hallo' and, with a final wave of his hand, they disappeared over the opposite slope.

Shadbolt envied him his compact little command, and thought bitterly of his two great lumbering convoys chugging helplessly over the countryside in the broad and dangerous daylight. He would have been still more bitter, had he known where they actually were! All that day he scoured the plain for some sign of the missing battery. The spectacle of a field officer, unshaven, unwashed and unfed, seeking vainly but pathetically for his command consisting of four heavy howitzers, four large caterpillar-tractors, twenty-odd lorries, some hundreds of rounds of ammunition and one hundred and fifty men—all lost in the open expanse that was Picardy—must have caused even the grave gods of war to smile.

That evening they were discovered by a spent, but still blaspheming B. C. The guns and tractors had overshot the mark and careered gaily on till they were stopped by an Infantry Colonel from charging his battalion headquarters in the line. Davies would probably have led them into the front trenches if the justly indignant Colonel had not been so insistent. It had been daylight by then, and too late to turn back in safety, so they had taken cover in a small wood about five hundred yards from the front line, where they mercifully escaped observation.

Lewis and his army had also taken a wrong turning in the dark and had wandered off into the area occupied by the neighbouring corps. On finding out his mistake he had caused considerable confusion, holding up the traffic of the whole Army Corps for several miles, by trying to turn his convoy to the right about on the narrow road.

The next six weeks were one continuous battle, punctuated by three more advances, till a position of stalemate was arrived at about the end of May. The final battery position was on the open hillside near Heninel.

The whole slope teems with men and guns. Vast dumps of shells, hundreds of small dug-outs, (mere shallow funk-holes in the ground), tents, cook-houses and latrines lie scattered over the countryside. The scene reminds one of a gipsy encampment on Epsom Downs before the Derby. The officers of 2 XX are sitting in the slightly larger hole, covered with elephant iron, which constitutes the mess. For the moment there is a blessed lull, and, as they finish tea, bare-headed, they stroll out to enjoy the peace and beauty of the summer evening. Only young Rawson remains behind. He wants to finish censoring the men's letters. *Crash! Ping! Ping!* The enemy is shelling the road with shrapnel twenty yards in front. Everyone starts to run for the dug-out, but before they reach it, the louder crash of H. E. sounds almost on them as a shell bursts through the flimsy roof of the mess. Shadbolt runs in, just in time to lift up poor Rawson, and to cushion his dying head with his arms.

Two days later Rawson's place was taken by another boy from England. Little Maitland was so small and innocent-looking that Hickling, with his passion for nicknames, immediately christened him 'Queenie.' The new subaltern had tiny hands and feet, and a complexion that any girl might have been proud to own, but within his small person beat a large heart, and although he had only just left school, he ordered the giant gunners about as if to the manner born.

Another scene in the same surroundings—Gunner Pope, the cook, a burly ruffian, whose face and hands and clothes are uniform in colour with his own stew-pots, is engaged in cooking the mid-day meal behind the shelter of corrugated iron, known by courtesy as the cook-house. Two satellites, only one degree cleaner than the Master himself, are busy peeling potatoes. Suddenly a large shell falls in the middle of the little group, and cook, potato peelers, dixies and stew-pots are sent flying. Gunner Pope extricates himself from under a heap of perforated iron sheets. Rising slowly to his feet, he ruefully regards the wreckage, 'That's the third time this week the spuds have been ruined by them blasted Allymands.'

A few days later the mess kitchen was hit and Shadbolt's batman, who was inside, was wounded. Shadbolt went to see him before he was taken off to the C. G. S. The faithful fellow produced what had once been a pair of nice-looking boots, the treasured relics of an ex-staff officer. They were riddled with splinters. 'I am sorry, sir,' he said, 'very sorry. If I'd 'a' known that the blinking kitchen was going to be hit, I wouldn't 'ave 'ad your best boots there.'

In May the enemy began to use a new fuse with great effect. Its instantaneous action caused the shell to burst directly it touched the ground sending a shower of splinters in a forward semicircle to a distance of several hundred yards. It was, of course, quite useless against dug-outs and shelters, but was extremely effective against troops in the open. In addition, shells fitted with the instantaneous fuse had a greater moral effect on account of the deafening crash of their burst. The arrival of a salvo can only be compared to the rapid rending of enormous tin tea-trays by some angry giant. They produced no shell hole. A lightly-scraped cavity in the ground was the only indication they left behind. The first time these arrived in the battery, Shadbolt rang up group headquarters to report that they were being heavily plastered with 8 in. or something bigger. When it was over, the Colonel came up to inspect the damage. He looked at the tiny cavities in the ground, sucked his moustache, and hinted pretty openly that one of his battery commanders was losing his nerve.

The next day Hickling was returning from the O. P. when he was pursued by a swarm of these terrifying hornets. Jumping breathlessly into a sunken road he nearly fell into the

General's car. There was no sign of the driver, but K. K. K. was sitting alone in the back, tranquilly eating his luncheon as if he were picnicking in some peaceful dell on a holiday tour in Devonshire. He offered Hickling a sandwich, and began to discuss the relative merits of beef and ham. Presently the shelling stopped, a scared-looking chauffeur picked himself out of the ditch, and K. K. K. drove on.

At the end of May, after one final scrap with the Colonel over the vexed question of ammunition returns, Shadbolt and 2XX left the Arras front and marched north to Ypres.

CHAPTER 6

Ypres And Messines—1917

In early June, 1917, the Ypres front was perhaps as peaceful as it had ever been since the beginning of that race to the coast which had ended in stalemate for the belligerents from the North Sea to Switzerland. To the war-weary warriors from Arras, the blood-soaked Salient seemed a very haven of rest and peace. The battery position was situated in a little copse, which formed part of the grounds of the Chateau des Trois Tours near Brielen, and in this sylvan retreat they settled down, happy in the expectation of a life of ease and leisured quiet. Little did they know that they were the forerunners of the mightiest concentration of artillery ever known in the world's history, and that, before the month was out, the opening phase of the greatest and most terrible battle of the war would have begun. Their pleasant dreams were rudely shattered in less than a week by the arrival of the first consignment of the vast quantities of shells which were to be used in the coming battles.

The organisation of the siege artillery into groups of batteries varying in numbers from two to ten, which was the system employed up to November, 1917, had several serious disadvantages. Each group was commanded by a Colonel, who, in times such as these, had barely got to know his Battery Commanders by name and the situation of their various batteries, when the whole group was reorganised, and he found himself as the nominal head of an entirely fresh set.

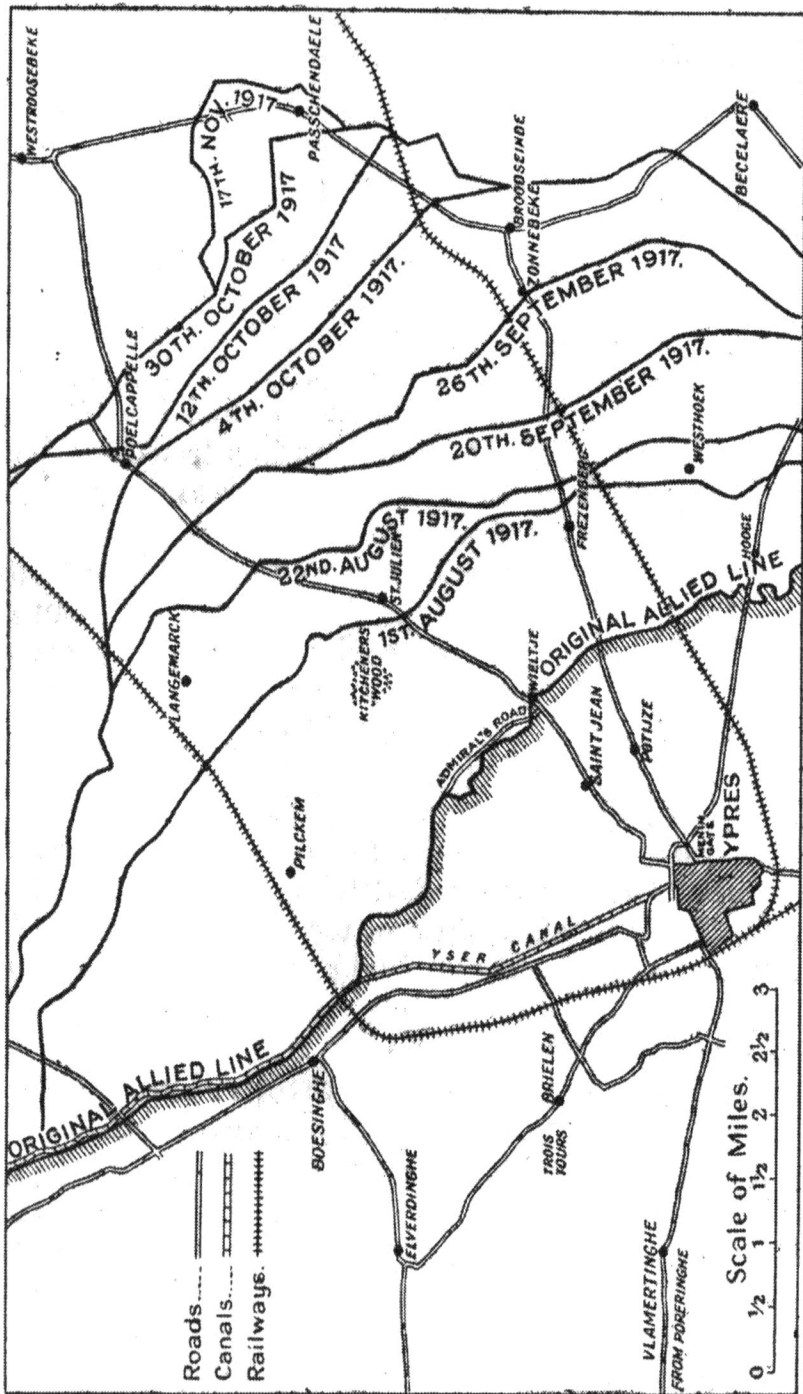

WESTROOSEBEKE

17TH. NOV. 1917

PASSCHENDAELE

BECELAERE

30TH. OCTOBER 1917

BROODSEINDE

12TH. OCTOBER 1917

ZONNEBEKE

4TH. OCTOBER 1917.

26TH. SEPTEMBER 1917.

POELCAPPELLE

20TH. SEPTEMBER 1917.

WESTHOEK

22ND. AUGUST 1917.

FREZENBERG

HOOGE

ST. JULIEN

1ST. AUGUST 1917.

ORIGINAL ALLIED LINE

LANGEMARCK

KITCHENER'S WOOD

ZILLEBEKE

ADMIRAL'S ROAD

SAINT JEAN

POTIJZE

PILCKEM

YPRES

YSER CANAL

ORIGINAL ALLIED LINE

BOESINGHE

BRIELEN

TROIS TOURS

ELVERDINGHE

VLAMERTINGHE

FROM POPERINGHE

Roads ....
Canals ....
Railways. +++++++

Scale of Miles.

0   ½   1   1½   2   2½   3

The words 'nominal head' are used here advisedly, for what chance had the most efficient C. O. of commanding, in any real sense of the term, a number of scattered units, whose position, personnel, armament, and numbers were changed about once a week. The siege battery, therefore, tended to become a self-contained command, and the B. C., like the Rajah of an independent state, was inclined to look upon all Colonels as emissaries of a superior foreign power, who must be placated and hoodwinked, or totally disregarded, according to the length of their stay and the force of their personality. To attain the maximum of efficiency, the various formations of the artillery, like the inter-dependent parts of a vast machine, must work smoothly together in a perfect accord of thought and action, but this was not possible under these unnatural conditions.

On arrival in the Ypres area, 2XX Siege Battery became part of the nth Heavy Artillery Group and, as soon as the battery was in action, the B. C. went in person to Group H. Q. to report to the Colonel. He seemed to be a pleasant and kindly old gentleman, with an intimate knowledge of the Salient. He gave Shadbolt a lot of excellent advice, and some even better beer, and, congratulating himself that at last he had got a C. O. whom he could respect and like, he returned to the battery. The very next day an entirely different Colonel appeared in the position, and announced that the battery had been transferred to his group. He was a much younger man than the C. O. of the day before, and far less human. Though the day was very hot, he declined the proffered refreshment, and at once launched forth into a long lecture on calibration and its effect on shooting. Tall and cadaverous, his nut-cracker face ornamented with a long drooping moustache, he theorised on the science of gunnery for nearly two hours. After the first half hour Shadbolt found it hard to pay attention. As in a dream, he heard the far-away monotonous voice saying 'ballistic coefficient—muzzle velocity—angle of projection—temperature of propellent—elimination of error,' and he woke with a start to find this zealous theorist was taking his departure. Needless to say, he did not inspect the position, nor take any interest in the practical working of the battery in action. Within a week his place was taken by another Colonel, who appeared in the battery daily in the role of kindly district visitor. He said a few comforting words to everyone, spoke hopefully of the prospect of leave, inquired after the men's health, and retailed any local gossip that he had collected on his rounds. He never talked 'shop' except with an apologetic air, as if he were some good-hearted bailiff sent by a remorseless landlord to demand the last instalment of the rent. That he was not lacking in humour, however, is proved by the following story. He had temporarily moved his headquarters into Ypres to enable him to obtain better control over his batteries during the coming battle at Messines. An Army Order had just been issued stating that all dug-outs in the Ypres area were at once to be made shell-proof. The Colonel had had a dug-out made for himself and his telephone exchange, and had roofed it with four new sheets of corrugated iron. The G. O. C. R. A. happened to pay him a visit and, noticing the new dug-out, said without a smile, 'Of course your dug-out is shell-proof, Colonel Maine.'

'It's better than that, sir,' replied the Colonel.

'How is that'? said the astonished C. R. A.

'It's rain-proof,' was the resourceful reply.

Next on the list of Colonels to take an interest in 2XX was one of the grandmotherly kind. He issued a little booklet to all the batteries in his group packed with detailed instructions, which covered every possible and impossible contingency. He was most particular about the safety of ammunition, and the prevention of fire. To this end, one of his orders read that a tub of water should be kept in each gun-pit, and another that instantaneous fuses should be kept separate from the ordinary delay action fuses. He came fussing into the battery position one morning, and without asking for the B. C., in itself a grave discourtesy if not an actual crime, walked into one of the gun-pits and began asking questions. The young sergeant-in-charge was a superior type of man, who prided himself on his knowledge of French.

'Now, Sergeant, let me see where you keep your ammunition,' said the Colonel. The sergeant showed him; the shells in one place, the cartridges in another, the fuses in a third, all according to orders.

'And where is your "Delay"?' said the Colonel.

The sergeant looked puzzled.

'I don't know about the *du lait,* sir,' he replied, 'but your *de l'eau* is in this tub.'

While 2XX were settling down in the grounds of the chateau, the bulk of the heavy and siege artillery on the Arras front had been brought up into the southern half of the Salient, to take part in the battle of Messines. Here, on a front half as long as that of Arras, were crowded an even greater accumulation of batteries. Twenty great mines, containing over 600 tons of explosives, had been driven into the long, low hill, which constitutes the Messines Ridge, and at 3.20 on the morning of June 7th, Shadbolt was awakened by a roar which shook his dug-out to its foundations.

Though the actual battle was taking place nearly seven miles away, his own guns had a long programme to fire in support of the northern flank, and he staggered out on to the position to superintend the working of the detachments. Far away to the south the sky was lit with flame, and, as he stamped his feet in the cold morning air, he prayed that at last a real victory might be granted to our arms.

By eight o'clock it was known that all the first objectives had been taken. Later, they heard that under the explosion of the mines and the downpour of shells, the whole of the German front line and its garrison had virtually disappeared, and that the moment our infantry surged forward under their canopy of fire, six miles of S O S rockets had risen from the German trenches in one long cry for help. At the end of the day, the whole of the coveted ridge was in our hands, and the most complete and absolute victory of the war had been consolidated.

This striking success was due to a number of factors, among which may be mentioned months of careful preparation and planning based on the bitter and costly experiences of the past, and a definite and limited objective. But, most important of all, was the concentration of sufficient artillery. Over three million rounds of ammunition had been expended, a million more than at the preliminary bombardment before Arras, and at Messines it was definitely and finally established that the heavy howitzer and not the machine gun, was the Mistress of the Battlefield.

Contrary to the teachings of the great military commanders of the past, it was accepted as an axiom at this stage of the war, that the achievement of the element of surprise in the delivery of an attack was out of the question. The stereotyped method of advertising the part of the line on which the impending assault would fall by a lengthy preliminary bombardment reached its climax at Ypres in 1917. From the middle of June to the end of July, the process of packing the base of the historic Salient with guns went on without cessation. Abandoning all hope of secrecy, the higher command crammed guns behind every hedge and wall, and into every field and street. In any case, every possible battery position in that small area was already well known to the enemy. They had been occupied by a succession of British batteries during the past two and a half years, and the German artillery had had ample opportunity of verifying and re-verifying their exact line and range. A large number of siege batteries was told off to engage the hostile artillery, which, owing to the open nature of the British preparations, had been concentrated in almost equal numbers by the opposing army. There developed, in consequence, throughout the month of July an artillery duel which exceeded, in magnitude and intensity, anything that had ever before been experienced on any front.

Shadbolt's battery was one of those that had been detailed for counter-battery work. Each evening the map location of the hostile batteries to be engaged was received from the Counter Battery Staff at Corps Heavy Artillery Headquarters, and each morning the aeroplane observer told off for the purpose, would signal the 'call sign,' which established his identity and notified his readiness to begin. The method of communication from the ground to the air was by means of strips of white cloth laid out on the ground in accordance with a recognised code. These were called 'ground strips,' and formed part of the equipment of the wireless operator who, with his receiving set, was attached to each siege battery on loan from the R. F. C.

Very definite and concise instructions were laid down for the effective co-operation between the R. F. C. and the artillery. Targets were located by aerial photography and subsequently engaged by aerial observation with the greatest success. In order, however, to attain complete understanding between the R. F. C. observer and the B. C., a close personal liaison was necessary. This was not always easy to achieve. The aerodrome was necessarily situated at least ten miles in rear of the gun positions, which made it difficult for both parties to find time to meet. Furthermore, the heavy casualties sustained by observers, as well as gunner officers, meant that the personnel of each arm was continually changing. Shadbolt's observer during this period was a gallant little officer, who made a point of dining with the battery at least twice a week. As if he had not had enough danger to face in the air during the day, he braved the terrible night drive from Poperinghe to Brielen, and arrived smiling in the mess like a jockey on a holiday. He never remembered to bring a gas helmet, such things not being necessary in the corps to which he belonged, and he never knew how to put it on properly when he was lent one. The battery was invariably shelled at least once during the meal, and a large quantity of gas shells generally formed part of the entertainment. The picture of little Devlin being assisted into his gas mask by three or four solicitous gunner officers, almost helpless with laughter and haste, remains as one of the lighter memories of those times. For now the artillery began to suffer such a tempest of hostile shell fire as they had never before endured in any previous battle. In every portion of the Salient, guns were being knocked out, shell dumps blown up, and fierce fires started by blazing cartridges and exploding fuses. The heavy casualties from gas and H.E. grew daily in number. Partly to cope with these and partly to economise in B. C.'s and staff new batteries from home were split in half, and the sections sent to separate batteries already in the line, which thus became six gun batteries with a personnel of about two hundred men.

On his way to the O. P. about 7.30 a.m. one morning, Shadbolt passed close to the cavalry barracks at Ypres and watched a six-gun battery of 9- 2 in. firing salvoes. It was a fine sight to see these six monsters in line all firing as one. About an hour later the enemy replied with eight batteries and for four hours rained down on them an incessant torrent of shells. When he returned about mid-day, four of the howitzers were standing on mounds of earth completely surrounded by shell-holes. The ground round the other two was not too cut up to prevent them being moved, but the gun barrels had so swollen with the intense heat of the enemy shells that they could not be run out of their cradles. All the ammunition had been blown up or destroyed, and the whole area was a welter of havoc and destruction. Fortunately the casualties amongst the personnel had been light, as the B. C. had withdrawn his men to a flank as soon as the heavy shelling had begun.

At Trois Tours the six 6 in. howitzers concealed amongst the trees were rapidly reduced to five and then four and then three. Night and day the shells burst in the little wood with a terrifying c-r-ump, and the casualties mounted and mounted. After dark the ammunition fatigues, the long programme of night-firing, and the incessant gas shelling from the enemy flayed ragged nerves and put an end to all thought of sleep. Even Hickling, the gay and imperturbable, was found wandering outside his dug-out one night muttering strange oaths and quite unconscious of where he was or what he was doing. Guns were knocked out and replaced to be knocked out again. The casualties and changes amongst the men were so numerous and continuous that Shadbolt ceased to know them all by sight.

Nevertheless, owing to the indefatigable gallantry and energy of little Devlin, and the resolution and endurance shown by all ranks amongst the gunners, the full programme of day and night firing was carried out without a break, and first in the list of successful shoots issued by the R. F. C. of the Third Army for July was the number 2XX.

The officer casualties were proportionately heavy. On one occasion there was only one subaltern left in the battery out of five. Shadbolt was notified that a reinforcement had been posted and might be expected that day. His name was Straker, and he had just been promoted from sergeant-major after two years' service in France. Shadbolt and Hickling were sitting in the stables of the chateau, which had been converted into a mess by the simple process of pulling a tarpaulin over the shattered roof and filling up the holes in the walls with sandbags. Hickling had turned on the gramophone to drown the sound of distant shelling, and was censoring the men's letters, Shadbolt was reading through the nightly budget from group headquarters, when a very youthful officer walked in. His large blue eyes under their long curling lashes, his brand new uniform, and general air of innocence, gave no clue to his identity or the reason for his sudden appearance.

'My name's Straker; I've come to join 2XX Siege Battery.'

Hickling burst into a roar of laughter, in which Shadbolt could not help joining. Shadbolt explained; 'I'm sorry we sound so rude, but the truth is we were expecting a much older officer, a ranker—'

'An old sweat with a row of drinking medals,' interrupted Hickling, 'not a blinking 'Eavenly Cherubim.'

The Cherub grinned. 'I came up in the train with another man called Straker, who answers to your description. We parted company at Poperinghe. I don't know what's happened to him.'

The Cherub's age in years was exactly 18½, but in experience of the world his appearance belied him. His knowledge of soldiering was nil, but when it came to command of language he might have given his namesake points in profanity and aptness. Coming straight from a public school to the salient, he compensated for his lack of training by his intelligence and his enthusiasm. Before he had been a week at Trois Tours he was slightly gassed, and had to be sent to the C. C. S.. for treatment. This, however, did not damp his ardour, and he returned ten days later to remain with the battery, as one of its most useful officers, until the end of the fighting. At the end of the month, a few days before zero day, the C. R. A. decided that the position at Trois Tours was untenable, and ordered Shadbolt to find another as near the old one as possible. There was no choice. The only unoccupied field was behind Machine Gun Farm, about three-quarters of a mile further south. Shadbolt sent off Hickling, the only remaining officer, with two guns and the wireless, while he, with the only remaining gun, stayed in action at the chateau. Just after dawn a telephone message came through from Group Head-Quarters, 'You are being called up on the wireless.' Asking Group H. Q. to telephone through all wireless messages as they were received, he rushed out on the gun to get everything ready.

It was only then he remembered that he had no 'ground strips.' A once white tablecloth was, after the gramophone, one of the most treasured possessions in the mess. Its dingy grey surface served to remind those who used it, of a civilisation which no longer formed part of their experience, but still lived in their minds as a dream, a dream of the distant and happy past. Sweeping away the preparations for breakfast, Shadbolt tore the tablecloth into four large strips and the shoot began. An hour later a large black cloud on the horizon bore sombre witness to its accuracy and effectiveness. The sequel to this shoot appeared three days later in the form of a curtly written memo from the Corps H. A. demanding an explanation in writing as to the cause of the delay in opening fire.

The new position was in an open field, whose virgin surface was marred by only two shell-holes, one large and one small, within about five yards of each other. Acting on the assumption that no shell ever falls exactly into the hole of a predecessor, Shadbolt put his B. C. post into the crater and the telephone exchange into its satellite. These were roofed over with elephant iron whilst the battery came into action to a flank and opened fire. Either by chance or design at the end of the shoot, the enemy immediately replied with a fierce burst of gun fire, and Shadbolt, who was talking on the telephone in the B. C. post, heard a loud detonation close at hand followed by an ominous silence. When he came out to investigate, he found the telephone exchange blown to pieces and the remains of two signallers lying scattered near the debris.

There comes a time when the limit of human endurance stretched to breaking point by major calamities, suddenly snaps at the impact of some minor one. Many men were shot for cowardice during the war, who in the past had faced great dangers and shown themselves possessed of a courage fully equal to that of their fellow men. On this occasion, Shadbolt and his B. C.A. ran without stopping until they reached the shelter of the neighbouring farm. Without speaking or looking at each other, they then returned at an abashed and reluctant walk to resume the duties they had so hurriedly abandoned.

The B. C.A. was a young man of about twenty-two, with a florid red face and twinkling brown eyes. He treated every contingency of war as a pleasantry devised by fate for his special entertainment and amusement. With his large mouth extended in a cheerful grin, this youthful mathematician used to juggle successfully with figures while the skies rained shells. Every subaltern in turn was taught his business by Bombardier Izod, and his buoyant personality and nimble brain were alike invaluable and irreplaceable.

His opposite number was a totally different type. Gunner Thomas was a Welshman, whose superior education had turned sour inside him. He suspected all those who were superior to him in military rank, if not in mental ability, of bearing him a personal grudge. All officers and sergeants came automatically under this category. His gloomy outlook on life contrasted forcibly with Izod's indomitable optimism. If it should be his turn on duty when Shadbolt entered the B. C. post in the morning, he would allow no smile of greeting to relax his melancholy features, but invariably produced some dismal prophesy about the weather or some well-founded complaint anent the discomforts of life in war time.

The bombardment of the German trenches and batteries increased in intensity from now until the 31st July, the date fixed for the advance of the infantry. During these final ten days approximately one hundred thousand tons of high explosives beat down on that desolate area of churned-up mud and slough, where a network of concrete islands sheltered the pent-up might of the German Army.

For here the ground was held by numerous disconnected trenches, and strong points arranged in depth rather than breadth. Scattered thickly throughout the system were small concrete forts known as pill boxes, whose cement and iron walls were strong enough to resist anything less than a direct hit from a 6 in. shell. These were garrisoned with machine guns, which fired through slits in the walls, and, when manned by determined men, formed obstacles that might well daunt the stoutest heart.

On the day fixed for the advance, another relentless foe to the Allies ranged itself once more on the side of their enemies. The weather, which up to now had smiled deceitfully, broke into a month of summer rain, adding one more obstacle to the attacking forces, an obstacle which, in the end, was to bring them to a standstill.

At four o'clock of a grey summer's morning, under a canopy of shell-fire and weeping clouds, twelve divisions moved forward to the attack, and by the end of the day had captured nearly all their objectives, including in the north, the Pilkem ridge and the village of St. Julien; in the centre, Verlorenhoek and the Frezenberg ridge; and in the south Hooge, Hollebeke, Stirling Castle and a line of woods. By mid-day the guns were already moving forward in support, the trenches were being spanned by light bridges, and the roads were thick with advancing traffic.

Shadbolt saw one battery come into action under heavy shell-fire in the open. Men and horses were falling fast, but the guns were brought into position and were soon replying with a steady fire. One poor driver, his legs hanging from his body by a thread and his entrails exposed to the pitiless rain, implored the sergeant-major to grant him that relief he was giving to the wounded and dying horses. After speaking to the obviously harassed officer in charge, the B.S.M. returned to satisfy the dying man's entreaty. Shadbolt turned his head away, thankful that the onus of responsibility had not been with him.

Most of the heavies did not move forward till the next night. It was still raining, and guns and howitzers had to be man-handled over the sodden spongy ground. Ever and again they would sink to their axles, and lines of tired, blaspheming men would heave and heave under the remorseless downpour. The blinding flash of a shell-burst would light up their glistening helmets and bowed forms and etched against the surrounding blackness, you saw a sudden picture of the slowly moving howitzer, the sandbags of the shattered trenches, the dismembered stumps of blasted trees, and caught the green shimmer of water in innumerable shell-holes. Straining at the ropes like beasts of burden condemned to unremitting toil, they would lose all fear of death in the hopeless misery of living, and when daylight broke, would sink to sleep in the mud, unmoved by shell-fire or by rain.

Shadbolt's battery advanced first into our old support line trenches and then into the former German front line system

MANHANDLING A 9·2-INCH HOWITZER AT PILCHEM, NEAR YPRES
14TH SEPTEMBER, 1917

near St. Julien. It was found impossible to accommodate the whole battery and its stores in the tiny area of broken water-filled trenches, and in addition, the hostile shelling was so intense and continuous, that no troops could remain there for an indefinite period without relief. A system which afterwards became common throughout the siege artillery was therefore adopted. Only sufficient officers and men to work the guns were kept in the battery, the battery office, the Q,.M.S. and his stores, and the reliefs remained in the rear position, which thus corresponded to the wagon-lines of the 60-pounders and the field artillery.

The difficulties of ammunition supply became more pronounced as the rain turned the churned-up countryside into a morass where wheels sank axle deep and animals laboured up to their hocks in clinging mud. Before the 31st July the task of the A. S. C. had not been a sinecure, for the only road from Poperinghe to Ypres was shelled every night by the enemy. The officer in charge sits in a lorry full of explosives, which, in the pitch dark, endlessly jolts forward, stops, and jolts on again like a London bus in a traffic jam. Sudden flashes momentarily light the roadside. He has an eerie feeling that he is being shelled with silent missiles from a noiseless gun, for the rattle and roar of the engines drown all but the nearest shell-bursts. The long column arrives without mishap at the road junction, where the Brielen-Renninghelst road crosses that from Vlamertinghe to Ypres, when the leading lorry skids heavily into the ditch. Cursing heartily, he orders the cargo of heavy shells to be unloaded, and with ears straining to hear the ominous whine of approaching shells, watches the frantic efforts of the men to get the lorry on the road again. This is done at last, the load replaced, and he heaves a premature sigh of relief. Then the next in the line skids into the same place. A column of mules and limbers going up with 18-pounder ammunition tries to pass, and is met by a battalion of utterly weary infantry marching down. With uncanny prescience the Boche chooses this inauspicious moment to put down his half-hourly concentration. Wild confusion ensues, a pandemonium of bursting shells, kicking mules and yelling men, the whole lit up in the glare of blazing cartridges, as a lucky shot sets fire to a lorry load. Finally, a harassed but ever cheerful A. S. C. subaltern arrives in the haven of the battery mess dug-out, swallows a much-needed drink, exchanges the news of the day, pockets his receipted tally and is off again on his dark and dangerous journey home. Probably his parting thought is 'Thank God, I'm not like those poor devils, condemned to live in this accursed spot.' And certainly their thoughts about him are 'What a life! Thank God we are safe and snug in our dug-outs, and are not compelled to go up and down those dangerous roads at night.'

After the advance, the roads in the forward area were impassable to long columns of lorries, and the heavy ammunition was sent up on light railways known as *'decauvilles'*. It was impossible to conceal the railway lines from the air, and these Were of course, frequently shelled. You saw the little train dashing down the track hotly pursued by bursting 5. 9's, its engine exuding oil, like a man in a sweat of terror, as it frantically puffed on its mad career. Some Canadian A. S. C. were running the *'decauville'* in Shadbolt's area. The number of shells on the train when it arrived at its destination never corresponded to the number on the tally. The shortage was so marked, that inquiries were eventually made as to what had happened to the balance. The reply was 'Why, we use those to fill up the shell holes and repair the track.'

Hickling left 2XX in August to take command of a battery of 8 in., and a new Captain was posted, named Merredew. Life in the forward position in front of St. Julien had become so unbearable that reliefs of officers and men took place every twenty-four hours. A new terror had been added to the constant crumping of 8 in. and 5.9's in the form of a very heavy howitzer, probably a 17 in. The first time it fired, Shadbolt and an elderly subaltern, known as Tipple, were sitting in the B. C. post of elephant iron and sandbag! A tremendous sound of *oo-oo-oo* was heard approaching.

'What on earth's that?' said Shadbolt.

'Pass the whisky,' said Tipple.

They each poured out a drink. Still the *oo-oo-oo-ah* getting louder and louder, filled the air. They had finished their whisky before, with a final *oo-oo-swish cr-rash*, this monstrous missile exploded into a mountain of mud and black smoke about two hundred yards in rear.

The rear position, where by this time some habitable dug-outs had been built, was shelled by a different kind of weapon, a high velocity gun, whose shell arrived without giving any notice of its coming. In fact, at a quiet time, you seemed to hear the distant report of the gun after the shell had burst. On the evening of Friday, the 13th September, Shadbolt, Tipple and the Cherub were sitting in the mess speculating as to where the next shot from this lightning gun would fall. Tipple was inclined to be gloomy. He pointed out the date and the day of the week, thereby unnecessarily emphasising the obvious, and asked the Cherub to pass the whisky.

At that moment a scared signaller put his head inside the dug-out, 'Please, sir, we 'aven't been through to the battery for nearly an hour. Sergeant Watson and a linesman went out on the line about 'arf past four, and the last we 'eard from them was that the shelling up there was somethink awful.'

Shadbolt ordered him to send two more linesmen to report to him at once. He reached for his helmet and gas mask and told the others that, whilst he went up to see what was wrong, they had better be prepared to bring up the reliefs. While they were yet speaking, two scarecrow figures almost fell down the dug-out steps . . . Merredew and Cooper from the battery. Their torn clothes covered with blood and dirt, their staring eyes and trembling hands bespoke disaster.

'The battery has been knocked out, twenty casualties, thirteen killed, all the instruments and maps gone west, two hows upside down . . . Oh! God . . . give me a drink.'

After a few minutes, the gaps in the story were filled up. About three o'clock that afternoon the Germans had begun to plaster the area with 8 in. Guns and howitzers were so closely packed along and in front of Admiral's Road, that casualties began to take place at once. Merredew and Cooper were binding up the wounded in the B. C. post, when a direct hit landed on the roof. There were ten men inside and instantly eight of them were blown to shreds. The other two, the two officers, staggered out from under a heap of human flesh, shattered sandbags and twisted iron, miraculously untouched. A few minutes later another shell landed on a detachment dug-out, killing all the occupants, and overturning the gun alongside. Merredew then withdrew the survivors to a flank. When the shelling moderated, he tried to get the battery into action again. The B. C. post was a shambles, all the instruments, maps, range tables and telephones had been destroyed. It was impossible to carry on, and for the first time in nine months 2XX was out of action.

The next morning Shadbolt and Tipple marched up with the relief detachments. They found naked torsos and portions of legs and arms jumbled together in inextricable and ghastly confusion. A common grave seemed the only solution to the grisly problem of burial, and in silence earth was heaped over the pitiful remains. The B. C. post was moved into a pill-box some distance to a flank, the guns were replaced on their platforms and by mid-day 2XX was firing again.

The Colonel came up a few days later and sent for Shadbolt in a towering rage. 'Why have I had no ammunition returns from you for a week? Why are they always wrong when you do send them in? Why are all your returns always late and always wrong? And why do you bury your casualties in the battery position? Can't you see how demoralising it is for the troops?' And the old gentleman stamped on the ground and glared at Shadbolt in righteous indignation.

Colonel MacDougall was a very senior colonel indeed. Unfortunately he had been passed over for promotion to Brigadier-general so often that his natural humanity had withered under repeated disappointments. His sole passion was returns. If only Battery Commanders would send these in accurately and up to time, honour and preferment for all concerned was assured. On this occasion, as on several others, Shadbolt patiently explained that the battery office containing all papers, war diaries and records had been blown up three times in Trois Tours, that the clerk had been killed and that his successor was a fool, but, unfortunately, the only man who could be spared. Touching the matter of the graves in the battery position, he had thought it more demoralising for the men to wrap the remains of their former comrades in sandbags for burial further afield, than to cover them reverently with earth where they lay. Besides, time was of importance, and the whole area was so packed with guns that burying further afield merely meant burying in some other battery position. The Colonel, however, refused to be mollified, but merely stumped away muttering, 'How could they hope to be successful in the field, if young officers like Shadbolt, who, in peace-time, would be no more than Second-Lieutenant, showed absolutely no grasp of essentials?'

Paradoxically enough, battle days on Admiral's Road were the most peaceful days for the gunners. The enemy artillery concentrated on the trenches and the advancing infantry, and only left a few heavy howitzers to deal with the attacking guns. The night before a battle was spent working out barrage tables in the evil-smelling little pill-box. At intervals the guttering candle would be blown out by the concussion from a nearby explosion or the threatening plop of gas shells would interrupt mathematics whilst respirators were put on and the men warned on the guns. Just before dawn, a copy of the completed tables was given to the No. I of each gun. This showed the angles and elevations and times for each successive lift. When the barrage began, all hope of issuing orders by word of mouth vanished, and a blast of the whistle, or a wave of the arm, was all that the officer on duty could achieve. On these occasions, the only casualties sustained were due to rare prematures from the 18-pounder gun muzzles immediately in rear. Six evil-looking mouths would spit and crack in deafening, unceasing clamour, and the shells pour over their bigger sisters like flocks of birds in whirring flight. To the right and left, in front and rear, a thousand others would join in to mingle their strident barking with the deep bellow and boom of the howitzers. First the bass and then the treble would lead the chorus until the whole swelled into a rending, rolling thunder of sound shattering the ether and annihilating thought.

At the end of the month 2XX was relieved. Fearful lest some further calamity should utterly destroy them, Shadbolt handed over quickly to his successor and marched his battered family down to rest billets in Poperinghe.

The casualties since June had amounted to over a hundred per cent. of the original battery strength. All the officers except the B. C. had been hit or gassed or sick, though some had returned to duty after a short spell in the C.C.S. In spite of these changes, the spirit of the battery as an individual unit remained unbroken. In those days, a unit, whose life history only covered a few months, was miraculously welded by battle into a corporate whole. Out of this ordeal by fire emerged an intangible spirit of fellowship, whose proud traditions would, under normal conditions, have taken years to build up. The tattered survivors of those terrible battles of 1917 marched out of the blood-drenched Salient with a feeling of spiritual exaltation which was never altogether to leave them. Knit by suffering, banded together in this awful freemasonry of Death, they might well exclaim, 'We few, we happy few, we band of brothers.'

CHAPTER 7

Cambrai—1917

The officers of 2XX decided to celebrate their first night out of the Salient by a champagne supper in the local estaminet at Poperinghe. Shadbolt was suffering from dysentery and felt too ill to eat, but being pressed by Merredew consented to try a little soup. Everybody was settling down to a happy evening when there was a tremendous crash, followed by the angry barking of some small gun.

'What was that?' said the Cherub. 'I thought we had left the war behind us.'

'I think it must have been a bomb,' replied Merredew, picking a red-hot splinter out of his soup. The droning hum of an aeroplane could be distinctly heard outside and three more detonations followed in deafening succession.

'It seems a pity to break up the party,' went on Shadbolt, 'but I think we had better go back to our billets and see if the men are all right. Tipple, we rely on you to bring along what is left of the champagne.'

That night the enemy planes paid three more calls and the following night they came again and the next and there was no sleep nor rest for the tired troops.

Shadbolt woke from an uneasy doze to be almost carried down into the cellar by the burly Tipple. Below in addition to the officers and batmen there were four civilians, one a very old woman who had become almost demented by fear. Shadbolt, still wrapped in his jaeger flea-bag, was propped against the wall, the others were standing in that taut silence which precedes the arrival of the next crash. Suddenly the old lady, with a scream of terror, flung herself at his feet and began praying to him in a chattering babble of French and Flemish. The cellar, its walls running with damp, the guttering candles, the scared faces, and the mad old woman were distorted by the sick man's fancy to form a vision grotesque and horrible. Stumbling he climbed the narrow steps to face the more familiar terrors of bombs bursting in the night.

On the fourth day he went to hospital, and the battery's 'rest' being over they entrained under Merredew's command for the Arras front.

It is possible that by this time the reader has received an impression of the Western Front as being in continuous eruption along its whole length. He sees a broad scar across Europe, aflame with gun-fire from end to end, lines of men advancing through the smoke of battle, farms and villages blazing, guns being blown up, horses and men dying in hundreds. This, of course, is a very exaggerated picture. There were many parts of the front which were almost as quiet as the peaceful English countryside, places where the crack of a solitary 18-pounder, or the occasional rip-rip of a machine gun were the only signs that a war was still in progress. It was to one of these peaceful spots that 2XX was now sent.

Shadbolt followed a few days later in the battery car. The morning was warm and sunny; one of those lovely October days which make you forget that summer is over, and that a long winter of mud and wet and aching cold is still to come. As the big Vauxhall sped down the long cobbled roads of Flanders and the distant rumble of gun-fire died away into silence, Shadbolt and the driver began to relax.

'It's a lovely morning, sir.'

'Fine', said Shadbolt.

'The old Pepper-Pot is running nice and sweet ain't she, sir?'

'Fine,' said Shadbolt.

'Shouldn't be surprised if she couldn't show some of these

'ere staff Daimlers a clean pair of 'eels. You don't mind if I shove 'er along a bit, do you, sir? I ain't 'arf glad to get away from that there Wipers.'

'Go on,' said Shadbolt, smiling, 'I'm pretty glad myself.'

Private Albert Inwards, A. S. C., was a fine driver and inordinately proud of his car. In the Salient the bodywork had become a mass of holes from shell splinters, and it had nearly broken his heart, but somehow or other the engine had miraculously escaped. Under continuous shell-fire he had nursed her over the worst roads in Europe, into shell holes, over dead mules and horses, and across country. Always cheerful and willing, he was ready to go anywhere from a run down to Poperinghe to fetch supplies for the mess, to a night trip up to Ypres, His only failing, if it could be called a failing, was a tendency to hum an unending, tuneless dirge when the road surface was sufficiently good, and his beloved car was running well enough to warrant this musical accompaniment.

Presently smoke stacks and slag heaps, and ugly mining villages gave way to real country, with trees and fields and little hills, all unscarred by war. Shadbolt felt as if a black cloud of care and depression had suddenly been lifted from his heart. The swelling curve of a ploughed field, the peaceful cawing of rooks, a patch of sun on some cottage roof, all brought a lump to his throat—a prayer of thanksgiving that God's green and lovely world still existed. Even Private Inwards *was* touched by this feeling of deep relief, for he broke into one of those melancholy songs about roses and home and mother, which denotes, all the world over, that the British Tommy is completely happy.

Shadbolt had lunch at the officers' club in Arras, a sunny, battered Arras, mysteriously empty and silent, and there learnt from a staff officer that 2XX was somewhere along the Cambrai Road, just beyond the village of Tilloy. They therefore drove along the broad and empty thoroughfare which leads in a dead straight line to Cambrai and Le Cateau, passed some heaps of broken bricks which might once have been a village, and, seeing and hearing no other signs of warfare, drove on. Private Inwards was expatiating on the peculiar habits of car-burettors when a sentry in a tin hat, gas mask at the alert and bayonet fixed, called upon them to halt.

'You can't go along 'ere, sir,' said the man. 'You'll be in full view of Jerry in another hundred yards.'

'Why, where are we now?' said Shad-bolt. 'Where is Tilloy?'

'These are the support line trenches, sir. Tilloy is about a mile further back down the road you've just come along.'

A quiet part of the line did not necessarily mean a quite time for the gunners. When battles were in progress batteries were responsible for a few hundred yards of front, whereas in a peaceful sector a heavy or siege battery might have to cover a frontage of a mile or more. O. P.'s had to be selected from which the whole of this country could be seen, and telephone communication established between them and the battery. In addition, alternative battery positions were chosen, and occasionally occupied, so that the enemy should be de-ceived as to the number of guns in the area. When Shadbolt arrived, an elaborate deception was in course of preparation by the Colonel of the Group to which 2XX had been affili-ated. A front of nearly three miles was being covered by only three batteries, comprising four 60-pounders and eight 6 in. howitzers. The Colonel had arranged that each gun should occupy one of twelve normally empty battery positions, and that they should all be connected by telephone to a temporary headquarters which had been established near Tilloy. On the night selected the Colonel would give the order to fire down the telephone, and from all over the countryside a rapid rate of gun-fire was to be opened on pre-arranged targets. The whole programme was carried through without a hitch, the only disappointing feature being that the enemy took no ap-parent notice of this unusual bombardment. However, when the Colonel, tired but satisfied, returned in the morning to his regular headquarters, he was gratified to find that a German

5.9 in. had scored a direct hit on his private dug-out, ruining his best pair of boots and reducing his bedding to rags.

A week or so later a big raid was carried out by the infantry near Monchy-le-Preux, and a number of siege batteries were brought in from other sections of the front to take part in the covering barrage. For about two hours a storm of shells was poured on to a few square yards of apparently unoccupied enemy territory, but the German artillery made no reply. About 5 o'clock the infantry walked over and brought back a few half-crazed prisoners, and the raid was over. To the battery fresh from the horrors of Ypres this kind of warfare was like spending a pleasant afternoon on the ranges at home.

The commonest form of deception practised by the artillery during the war was the concealment of guns and battery positions from enemy aircraft. In the early days guns were painted in bold irregular patches or covered with branches of trees, to make them assimilate with their surroundings. This was all that was necessary to conceal them against direct visual observation, but with the introduction of aerial photography the technique of camouflage grew in importance. The airman's eye might not be able to detect the presence of guns even when flying over them at 1,500 feet, but a photograph taken from 4,000 to 6,000 feet would reveal their location unless the whole area was carefully camouflaged. The interpretation of aeroplane photographs became a highly skilled work, on which specially trained men were employed on the counter battery staffs. It must be understood that the picture of the gun itself was never produced. Its presence was deduced from one or other of the following effects.

1. The black shadows cast by the guns or their emplacements.

2. The break-up of surroundings due to alterations in surface caused by gun-pits and dug-outs.

3. The tracks leading up to battery position.

4. The 'blast' marks immediately in front of the guns

caused by the scorching of grass through firing. Burnt grass has fewer shadows on its surface than unburnt, and consequently appears lighter in tone on a photograph.

5. All newly-dug earth. This shows up white in photography, because, having no shadow casters, such as grass, its surface reflects light rays readily.

Thus, the problem for the gunner how best to conceal his guns, became one of counteracting by artificial means these effects of light, shade, and tone in aerial photography, which from interpretation arid inference might reveal the location of his battery to the enemy. Early in 1917 a camouflage officer was appointed to the heavy artillery of each corps, who was responsible for the issue of special camouflage material to batteries, and was always ready with technical advice as to its disposal. The material mainly consisted of rolls of wire and fish netting on to which small strips of coloured canvas had been knotted, and bundles of material of a canvas texture called 'scrim.'

The wire netting was erected on poles and supported over the gun and its emplacement, the object being to create a perfectly flat overhead cover which in plan should symmetrise with the surroundings, and conceal the black shadows cast by the gun and other objects in or near the pit. This cover aimed at the production of another surface which should have the effect of absorbing and reflecting about the same amount of light as the surrounding grass, and consequently appear of the same tone in the photograph.

The scrim was used to throw over guns, shell dumps and earth works without employing any form of structural support. This method was only efficacious on broken ground, amongst ruins, and under trees where there were already sufficient irregularities of surface to ensure the production of plenty of black shadows, so that the addition of a few more would excite no suspicion.

From a B. C.'s point of view the expenditure of time and

thought on the concealment of a battery position was perhaps even more important in a peaceful sector than in battle areas. The chances of the enemy selecting your battery for a day's shoot were enormously increased when it was the only one in action on a wide front. A great deal of work was, therefore, put into the concealment of 2XX's new position. To hide the blast marks Shadbolt borrowed a horse and plough from an astonished civilian, and ploughed up the ground for a considerable distance in front of the guns. All tracks leading to the guns, B. C. post and detachment dug-outs were carefully obliterated and strict orders issued to prevent the formation of new ones. This was not, of course, an easy matter, but in this instance the difficulty was solved by digging narrow trenches, 6 foot deep, from the road to the line of guns, removing the earth dug up and spreading it on the plough, and covering over the top of the trenches with camouflage netting so that it blended with the surrounding grass. Dug-outs for the reliefs, the Q. M. S. and his stores, officers' quarters, cook-houses, and the signal exchange, in fact all the non-combatant half of the small township which comprised a battery in trench warfare, were built some distance to a flank, and also elaborately camouflaged. When everything was finished, the R. F. C. were asked to take an aeroplane photograph, but before the negative could be developed, 2XX was ordered to move.

East of that section of the line which extends from Bullecourt in the north, to Villers Guislain in the south, lies the important town of Cambrai. Situated seven miles behind the famous Hindenburg Line, whose barbed wire entanglements, well-sited trenches, and deep-mined dug-outs were object lessons in the strength and impregnability of modern field-works, Cambrai dominated the railway communications of the German Army. It was here, therefore, that a surprise attack had been planned by the British General Staff. The arrangements for the attack comprised several novel features, chief among which were the absence of a preliminary artillery bombardment and the massed advance of four hundred tanks. In order to ensure secrecy no orders were issued for the attack, nor were units even informed that an attack was going to be made until the day before it took place. The flotillas of tanks were assembled by night in Havrincourt Wood and every possible place which offered cover from aeroplane observation. A large number of guns were brought down to the area and placed in 'silent' positions. No firing was permitted on any account, for fear of rousing the enemy's suspicions. Although no preliminary registration was allowed, on the day appointed the tanks and infantry moved forward behind a barrage which equalled in accuracy and effectiveness the carefully registered bombardments of earlier battles. The batteries, which had been rushed out to France in the early part of the year, had completed their training in the hard school of war. The value of 'meteor' correction and careful calibration was now fully appreciated by those battery commanders, who, nine months earlier, would have scoffed at these methods as being too scientific and theoretical for practical use.

On the morning of November 20th 2XX was in action just north of the Bapaume Road, and an observation post had been established about two miles to the southeast in a traverse of our front-line trench. The night had been spent in working out the calculations for the next day's barrage, and perfecting the arrangements for keeping in touch with a forward observer (F. O. O.) should the attack be successful. It had been decided that Tipple should go over with the infantry, taking with him two signallers and a lamp so that communication with the O. P. in the old front-line trench could be maintained, and fire brought to bear on any point which held up the infantry in their advance.

An hour before dawn Shadbolt walked up over the rolling grassland which led from the battery to our trenches. The picket lights of numberless batteries twinkled like little stars in the darkness, and the silence of the night was broken by the murmuring movements of hundreds of unseen men. Away to the right the black bulk of Havrincourt Wood loomed large against the sky-line, and from within its sombre depths came the irregular crack and spit of cold engines followed by a pulsating roar as each tank moved forward into its battle position. He stepped down into the communication trench and pushed his way through the lines of armed men, some talking in low voices, others joking and laughing, some silent, but all waiting in tense expectancy for the sound of that first gun which should send them forward into the Unknown. Tipple was waiting for him in the O. P. with the signallers. His normally red face was a shade redder in the early morning cold, as he poured out a generous tot of rum for himself and his men. The last arrangements were made, the line to the battery tested for the twentieth time, and there was nothing to do but wait and stare expectantly at the little funnels and wisps of mist swirling and eddying over the silent land beyond the parapet.

At twenty past six of a grey and hazy autumn morning, under cover of a dense barrage of gas and smoke, the long line of tanks waddled slowly forward, closely followed by silent columns of bayoneted infantry. As the back of the last man vanished into the fog, and the reply of the enemy guns came crashing behind them, Shad-bolt wondered what would be the outcome of this, the fourth great battle of that eventful year. When the early morning mist had cleared away it soon became obvious that the first advance was an unqualified success, and that the Germans had been taken completely by surprise. Having cut great swathes in the wire, the tanks had dropped bundles of faggots from their bows into the open trenches, and moving forward over these, had broken up the machine gun nests and enfiladed the astounded inmates. The eager infantry had followed to complete the work. Within a few minutes the Hindenburg Line along a front of six miles had been captured, and the assailants were moving forward against the strongly fortified tunnels of the Reserve Line. By half-past ten this was also in our hands, and the British troops, with cavalry close behind, were advancing to their final objective in open country.

Up to this hour Shadbolt had received a number of requests for fire from Tipple's winking light, and these were passed down by telephone to the battery. Before mid-day, however, orders were received from H. Q. to cease fire, and at the same time the signallers reported that they were unable to get in touch with the F. O. O.'s party. As hour after hour went by and no news was received from them, Shadbolt became very anxious. Just before dark, fearing the worst, he gloomily returned to the battery position. Despite the great successes of the day, the officers of 2XX sat down to the evening meal with heavy hearts.

Stories of Tipple's unfailing courage and serenity, of his unselfishness and endless good temper, passed from mouth to mouth.

'Do you remember, Major,' said the Cherub, 'that first night I arrived at Trois Tours? It was Tipple who took me into his dugout and gave me a shake-down for the night. And when the Boche started shelling the old man woke me up and insisted on helping me with my gas mask before he put on his own. After that he talked the whole time in case I should be frightened, and you know what slobbery things gas masks are to talk in?' His weaknesses and lovable little failings were not forgotten.

'Yes, and do you remember, Cherub, when we were sharing that dug-out with him on the canal bank,' went on Cooper; 'there was over two foot of water slopping about on the floor, and we had to get in and out of bed in gum boots, and the first night old Tipple drank the whole of our rum issue as well as his own? Had a cold coming on, so he said. When we found out we damn nearly killed him.'

At that moment the blanket was lifted from the dugout entrance and in walked Tipple.

'Evening, everybody. Pour me out a drink, Cherub, I've had the hell of a day.'

'Damn and blast you, Tipple,' broke out the Cherub. 'What do you want to come breaking in here for like that? We all thought you were dead.'

'Tell us all about it, Tipple,' came from a chorus of voices.

'Well, you see, everything went wrong from the start. A bullet went through my flask, the moment I climbed over the parapet. I felt a bang on the hip, but didn't think anything of it in the excitement. It wasn't until I got into the Reserve Line that I discovered the flask was empty, and that I must have left a trail of whisky the whole way from our front line. I went down into one of those big tunnel dug-outs. Lord, they're marvellous! Tables and chairs, electric light, and rows of bunks just like a ship. There were one or two dead Boches, and I found a lock of a woman's hair and some hairpins, but not a drop to drink.

'Then I wandered on with some infantry coves I had got pally with, and we had a private scrap with a German officer and four men with a machine gun. They fought like the devil, and by that time I had lost touch with you, Major, and couldn't help things out with a few rounds of H. E. However, we settled them in the end, and I got the officer's periscopic glasses. Then I thought I would push off a bit further south where there was some rising ground from which I hoped to be able to signal back to the O. P. again. I must have got very nearly to Flesquieres. Our infantry were being held up by machine gun fire, and the Boche had got one or two field guns pushed right forward to take on the tanks. There was one battery in action at the bottom of the slope. Only one gun was firing, the rest had been knocked out, but this one was doing wonderful work. Our tanks were advancing more or less in single file, and every time a tank breasted the hill and appeared on the sky line, bang went the Boche gun and laid it out. I saw at least twelve tanks lying about the hillside and there may have been more. As far as I could see with my glasses, at the end there was only one man left alive on the gun, and he was loading, laying and firing it by himself. He looked like an officer, but whoever he was, he was a stout fellow. By this time I was nearly mad at not being able to get through to any of our own artillery, so I thought I had better walk back a bit, and report the situation to any battery or senior gunner officer I could find. I eventually found some 18-pounders and told them all about it. Had a drink with them, and as I couldn't do any more to help, began to make tracks for home. I lost my way and walked about twenty miles. Gunner Sullivan collapsed, and I had to carry his lamp and rifle and kit for him, and here I am.'

The next day the battery moved forward to a position south of the Bapaume road in order to take part in the further attack of the infantry. At the end of the week the net gains were over 10,000 prisoners, 142 guns and more than sixty square miles of territory, including ten villages. The joy-bells had hardly ceased ringing in London when Ludendorff made his counter stroke. On Friday, the 30th, the enemy attacked at both ends of the re-entrant which had been made in his line by the British advances. In the south he advanced as far as Gouzeaucourt, and captured some field batteries at La Vacquerie, the first British guns to be lost since April, 1915. In the north he employed an even larger force in a fierce thrust against Moeuvres and Bourlon Wood, but here he was not so successful.

The day was starred with heroic deeds. It was between Moeuvres and the Canal du Nord that a company of infantry found itself isolated and completely surrounded. At 4 p.m. the two remaining officers, the company sergeant-major, and the platoon sergeants held a council of war, and unanimously determined to fight to the last. The two runners who were sent back to notify this decision succeeded in getting through to battalion headquarters. During the remainder of the afternoon and far into the night this gallant company were heard fighting, but no help could be given, and it is presumed that they were eventually overwhelmed and died to a man. In one 18 pounder battery five men and an officer served three guns at point-blank range, the trails almost crossing as they covered three separate fields of fire. Cooks, runners, orderlies, and staff officers in pyjamas, all threw themselves into the fight, and eventually the oncoming tide was stemmed. On December 7th the British line was withdrawn to the Flesquieres Ridge, so that the whole salient was smoothed out, the fighting died down, and 2XX returned to its original position between Beugny and Morchies, about 1½ miles north of the Bapaume-Cambrai road.

The system of grouping siege batteries in batches, the size of which varied according to the exigencies of the military situation, came to an end at the close of the year. Batteries were brigaded in groups of four, usually three 6 in. howitzer batteries and one 9*2 in. or 8 in. battery. Henceforth, the Colonel of the Brigade, the Adjutant, and the headquarters staff, and the four batteries were to move and fight as one unit, and remain together for the rest of the war. In the peaceful sector where, after a year's fighting, 2XX had apparently Settled for the winter, Shadbolt awaited with some misgiving the arrival of the new Colonel. Someone has said—it was either Napoleon or General Crozier— 'There are no bad troops, only bad Colonels.' Would this one be a 'spit and polish' enthusiast, a zealot for accurate ammunition returns, a believer in endless gun and rifle drill, because they were in a quiet part of the line, and the men must, at all costs, be kept busy, or merely a nonentity without even sufficient character to act as a buffer between his batteries and the Generals who occasionally prowled round in peaceful times like these?

Colonel Carp turned out to be none of these things. On the contrary, he was that rare type of soldier whose boundless energy and enthusiasm were guided by common-sense and human sympathy, and whose real knowledge of his profession was untrammelled by professional tradition and red tape. Shadbolt soon discovered that the new Colonel's whole individuality was entirely concentrated on one object, the winning of the war, to which end the efficiency and well-being of his batteries were important subsidiaries. He contrived, however, to hide these excellent qualities under an abrupt, shy manner, and could make himself extremely unpleasant if things were not done exactly in accordance with his wishes and in the way he laid down.

Shadbolt was sitting in the B. C. post one morning, super-intending the construction of a brick fireplace, which should make the dug-out more habitable during the long winter nights, when Bombardier Izod came in.

'The Colonel is in the battery, sir. He is talking to Mr. Straker on No. 1 gun.' He looked out and saw a little man in a large pair of spectacles speaking very emphatically to the Cherub. As he approached he caught the end of what was evidently a customary homily.

'Now, my boy, there are only three possible answers to my question, "Yes," "No," or "I don't know." In this case you ob-viously don't know, so why try to cover up the fact with a long story?'

Shadbolt walked forward and saluted.

'Ah! good morning, Major Shadbolt. Can you tell me the lot number of the last batch of the 106 fuses you received?'

'I'm afraid I do not know, sir, off-hand, but—'

'That is all I want,' said the Colonel, his eyes beaming be-hind their glasses, 'I've no doubt you can spin me a long yarn about them, but all I want in answer to any question is "Yes," "No," or "I don't know." Is that clear? Now take me to your B. C. post, I want to telephone to my headquarters.' Seizing the telephone he began, 'Colonel Carp speaking —who is that? What do you mean, Hullo? Haven't I told you a hundred times I will not have anyone say "Hullo" on the telephone? Oh, is that you Butler? The lot number of those fuses is C10672.'

When he finally walked away, his little bow legs going at full speed, as he hurried to the next battery, he left the officers of 2XX feeling rather shattered.

'Well,' said the Cherub, 'so much for the new Colonel. Carp by name and carp by nature. God help us.

'Oh, shut up, Cherub. The only thing he complained about was your own fault. I was going to tell you off about it myself, only the Colonel got there first. All the same, it looks as if we were going to spend most of our winter's rest battling with this human dynamo.'

Shadbolt's diagnosis turned out to be incorrect, for a period of happy peace now set in for those batteries in the Morchies area, a peace which remained unbroken until the great German offensive in March, 1918. Peace meant a regular programme of day and night firing, constantly harassing the enemy's lines of communication, the roads, tracks and trenches which led to his front line, and the batteries, headquarters and strong points which were revealed by aeroplane photographs.

It also entailed a great deal of work in the construction of dug-outs and telephone systems. But it did not mean much heavy shelling from the enemy, and, as the work progressed, time was found for the reliefs to play football in rear, and for some of the officers to motor to Amiens to do the Christmas shopping.

The year 1917 had seen another big increase in the number of heavy and siege batteries in France, actually 338 guns had been landed, compared with 900 in the previous year, bringing the grand total up to 1,584. The obsolete 4.7 in. and 6 in. 30 cwt. had all been withdrawn, and their batteries re-armed with the 60-pounder and the 6 in. 26 cwt. The expenditure of ammunition had been enormous. During the seven weeks' fighting at Arras, 6¾ million rounds, weighing approximately 169,000 tons, had been poured out on the enemy trenches and batteries. At the Messines battle 3¼ million rounds, weighing 85,500 tons, and costing nearly 17 million pounds, had been expended in a week. At Ypres 2 million shells were fired weekly from the 30th July to the 7th October. This compares with an average expenditure over the whole front of about 70,000 rounds a week during the last six months of 1916 when the battle of the Somme was raging. But the greatest change had taken place in the batteries themselves. From heterogeneous collections of semi-trained men, led by youthful and inexperienced officers, they had been moulded by war into composite units. Their technical training had been completed on the battlefield. In addition, they had acquired that power of grappling with emergencies, and of making the best of every contingency, which is the hall-mark of seasoned campaigners.

The year which had begun with such high hopes for the Allies ended on a note of disappointment and foreboding. The sudden and absolute breakdown of

Russia, involving Roumania in ruin, the collapse of the Italian Army, and its subsequent retreat to the Piave, had more than offset the exhausting victories of Arras, Messines, Passchendaele and Cambrai. The whole force of Germany and Austria, together with a quantity of captured Russian and Italian artillery, was now available for the Western War. From the Baltic to the southern frontiers of Russia, troop trains, laden with infantry and guns, were converging towards France, where Ludendorff was preparing that final and decisive stroke which should bring victory or defeat to the German arms.

CHAPTER 8

The Retreat—1918

All unconscious of the desperate days to come, the batteries in front of Beugny passed a quiet and happy winter. The long walks to the O. P.'s over the open rolling country were as devoid of incident as tramps over the Yorkshire moors; a hostile shell in the battery position was an event. An old-fashioned Christmas, with snow on the ground, was spent in feasting and in merry-making, including a real Christmas dinner for the men, with roast pork and beer, and packets of cigarettes from home.

Early in the New Year the whole Brigade pulled out for a rest at Gezaincourt, near Doullens. It seemed ironical that the only occasion on which 2XX was taken out for a rest was at a time when no fighting was in progress, no casualties had been sustained, and the battery had been sufficiently long in one place, to make the position their home. Shadbolt was at Corps Headquarters at the time, acting for the Heavy Artillery Brigade-Major who was on leave. Life on the staff did not seem to have changed for the better since 1915, and directly the Brigade-Major returned, he applied for leave himself. This was readily granted by the C. R. A., but Colonel Carp wired from the rest camp, 'Regret leave impossible. State of your battery demands your immediate return.' Shadbolt motored back over the old Somme battlefields, wondering gloomily what Merredew had been doing to warrant this peremptory message. Hugh was a good fellow, but no soldier, too vague and casual. There was that time at Ypres when he set off one morning from the rear position to relieve Shadbolt at the battery. He never turned up and was eventually discovered, at night-fall, in an abandoned O. P., composing poetry, under the mistaken impression that he had been ordered there for the day. Then there was that story of him before the war. How he had booked a passage to go to America, but on arriving at the quayside conceived a sudden dislike for the appearance of the boat. Wandering aimlessly along the docks, suit-case in hand, he saw a ship he liked better, so he strolled on board—and went to China instead. He must have done something pretty serious this time to make the Colonel so annoyed. Still, in spite of his vagueness, Hugh was such a lovable character that no one could be annoyed with him for long. Private Inwards, who had come to fetch Shadbolt, seemed curiously depressed. Although the road from Albert onwards was a good one, his usual cheerful humming was conspicuously absent. Arriving at Gezaincourt, Shadbolt went straight to the Adjutant's office.

'What's the matter with the Colonel, and what on earth's wrong with my battery?'

'Well, you see, sir, the Colonel hates being in rest. He can't get on with the war from here, so he works off his feelings on the batteries. Yesterday he told Merredew that your car was filthy, and poor old Hugh replied that you always kept it like that, but he was willing to bet an even fiver that it would give the Brigade car a five furlong start in a race to Amiens and back. The Colonel was speechless. He came straight in here and sent you that wire. I think you will find that things have quietened down by now.'

When the Brigade returned to Beugny, preparations were already in progress for an elaborate defensive system. A reserve line known as the Brown Line was being dug about three thousand yards behind the front, and behind that again a Red Line, an old enemy trench, was being repaired and fortified. During the next two months the preparations for the artillery defence were completed. All the battery positions and O. P.'s were constructed to cover both the Brown and the Red Lines. This meant a great deal of hard work, as six gun-pits had to be dug at each position, wooden platforms laid, camouflage erected, command posts sunk in the ground and drained, and hundreds of rounds of ammunition dumped. Elaborate orders were issued laying down the targets and rates of fire in the event of an enemy attack. These arrived from Corps Heavy Artillery almost daily, and after numerous additions and amendments, and additions to amendments, and amendments to additions, they took the form of a fairly lucid five page document, issued on the eve of the battle, which covered every possible and impossible contingency.

Broadly speaking the artillery defence was divided into two phases, counter-preparation and S.O.S. The first was intended to break up the enemy's forces whilst massing for the attack, the targets being chiefly communication and support trenches, and road junctions. The second was a barrage across No Man's Land which should annihilate the German infantry as soon as they left the shelter of their trenches. The recognition of this fateful moment being all important, careful arrangements were made for a system of signals should telephone communications be destroyed by hostile shell-fire.

On the evening of March 20th a despatch rider arrived at Brigade Headquarters with a hastily prepared map of the German forward areas in the sector. It was covered with little black dots.

'What are those?' said the Adjutant.

'German guns in the open,' replied the Colonel grimly, 'spotted by the Flying Corps only two hours ago.'

At the same time the nightly Corps Summary of Information, amplified the Colonel's assumption.

A special reconnaissance of the area between Moeuvres and Inchy from 2.30 p.m. to 4 p.m. to-day reports a number of suspected new gun positions and material in the open. No guns were actually seen, but objects covered by tarpaulins were observed. Accurate location was difficult owing to the clouds and the large number of objects seen.

Shadbolt retired early to his dug-out that night. The strain of waiting for the long deferred attack was beginning to show in fretted nerves and shortened tempers. Even the cheerful Cherub had been rather morose at dinner.

He woke with a violent start, conscious of noise, intense, incessant, unmistakable. The ground shook, the bed vibrated, and every few seconds a nearer concussion brought down handfuls of earth from the roof. Shadbolt felt for his torch. It was five o'clock. Seizing the telephone he buzzed up the exchange.

'Give me the B. C. post. Is that you, Izod? Where's Mr. Cooper?'

'He's on the guns, sir. They're firing counter-preparation.'

At that moment the dug-out door was blown from its hinges and a hundred yards away in the little valley below, through a cloud of drifting smoke and dust, he saw the six squat noses of his howitzers rise in line from their pits, belch out six flaming tongues of fire, and slowly disappear again. Stately and imperturbable, again they nosed gently up, and their crashing salvo could be clearly heard above the noise of the bursting shells. He felt for his gum-boots, put on his coat and hat, grasped the gas mask lying by the bed, and staggered out into the reeking daylight. Outside, the whole face of the earth was changed. Where there had been green grass and a level track, lay hundreds of smoking shell holes. Great fountains of earth kept springing up between him and the battery, and the noise of their spouting deafened his senses. In front, six bright flashes stabbed again through the smoke. He reeled in the blast of a monstrous explosion. A giant hand hit him full in the face. He remembered no more.

Meanwhile, Merredew had safely reached the B. C. post which was dug into the opposite bank of the shallow gully in which the guns were in action. The telephone lines to the

148

O. P., to the rear position, and to Brigade Headquarters had all been cut, and parties of signallers had already gone out to repair them.

No mention of the work of the artillery during the war would be complete without a tribute to these gallant men. Wherever the shelling was heaviest, they were to be found with tape and spare wire, repairing the vital nerve threads between the guns and their eyes at the O. P. They usually worked in pairs, but were often alone, patrolling up and down the long stretches of line which led from the battery, sometimes into No Man's Land itself. Others sat cramped in some narrow dug-out, or evil-smelling trench, endlessly tapping and buzzing and halloing down that most maddening of all man's inventions, the telephone.

Failing to get through to Brigade, but hearing reassuring news from the O. P. Merredew continued on the counter-preparation targets. By seven o'clock the shelling round the battery had almost ceased, though the noise of heavy gun fire in front had by no means diminished. The reliefs were brought down, and the night crews sent to breakfast. An hour later the enemy barrage burst with renewed fury on the hapless gully, but owing to the gun-pits being well sited under the shelter of the forward bank, little damage was done and no casualties were sustained. The only telephone line that was working, the one to the O. P., was again cut, and it was not until half-past ten that communication with the outer world was re-established. A runner, who had been sent to Brigade Headquarters in Beugny, returned with the order to fire on the S.O.S. targets at the normal rate. At half-past eleven the O. P. reported 'Enemy advancing on Lagnicourt. Large bodies of infantry, cavalry, and tanks on right of Pronville,' and half an hour later Tipple, with four signallers, arrived from the O. P. reporting that the enemy had broken through, and that he had only just had time to get away before being surrounded. By this time the enemy shelling had entirely ceased and Merredew collected his officers for a council of war. It was decided that Cooper should man a reserve O. P. about half a mile in front, whilst Straker and Maitland collected every available man, including all infantry stragglers, and posted them in shell holes on the flanks of the battery with the two Lewis guns and such rifles as could be produced. Merredew himself would superintend the arrangements from the roof of the mess dug-out where he had a good view of the surrounding country, to a range of over 2,000 yards. From here he could keep in touch with Cooper by lamp and flag, and shout through a megaphone to Tipple on the guns, any orders that the situation required.

'What's the news of the Major?' said the Cherub.

'He's in the rear position, sir,' replied the sergeant-major, 'still unconscious and breathing 'eavy.'

'Is he fit to travel?' asked Merredew.

'Well, I can't find no mark on 'im, sir, I think he's just concussed-like.'

'Put him in the car, and tell his servant to put his kit in with him, also the mess gramophone. Tell Private Inwards to drive as gently as he can, and not to stop for anybody until he gets to Albert where he's to report to the nearest Field Hospital.'

'Very good, sir.'

A period of ominous quiet now set in, only broken by occasional winking messages from Cooper that our infantry were streaming past him, but no Germans were to be seen. Indeed, numberless infantry stragglers soon began to appear in the battery, mostly walking wounded, and were rounded up by Straker and Maitland into some semblance of a defensive force. Meanwhile all the shells in the gun-pits were fused with the instantaneous 106 fuse, and everything got ready for a fight to the finish.

At half-past one, large bodies of Germans were reported on the ridge west of Lagnicourt, and these soon appeared in view of the battery, moving south-west towards Morchies. They were at once engaged over open sights, Merredew calling the ranges from his post on the mess roof, and the gunners watching for the first time their own shells bursting—bursting

6-INCH GUNS RETIRING THROUGH THE OLD SOMME BATTLEFIELDS
MARCH, 1918

on an oncoming enemy whose columns halted, broke up and then turned and fled. Half an hour later the enemy massed for a further attack, this time north of Lagnicourt, and were again driven back in disorder, many casualties being inflicted.

At three o'clock, Cooper reported the Germans advancing in waves down the valley towards the Noreuil-Morchies road, and at the same time stated he was forced to evacuate the O. P. owing to machine gun fire, and the fact that he was becoming isolated without any infantry in front of him. Merredew opened fire on the advancing masses and again had the satisfaction of seeing them scatter and run back over the sky-line towards Lagnicourt.

Cooper returned in safety, and at four o'clock another more determined attack developed from the same direction. Heavy machine gun fire was brought to bear on the gully, and an enemy field gun was run up into the open and began firing at a range of about i,200 yards. The enemy massed in great quantities, and, on being engaged by the howitzers, split up into small parties, and advanced towards the Brown Line. The field gun was silenced with two salvos, but it was difficult to stop the advance of the small parties, some of whom reached the Brown Line and entered Maricourt Wood, four hundred yards from the position. They were, however, engaged and eventually beaten off with rifle fire from Maitland's party. In all, eight hundred rounds were fired that day from the howitzers of 2XX, the lowest range being 1,000 yards.

In the evening a message came by runner from Brigade. 'Batteries will retire to positions covering Brown Line.' But Merredew was tired. It was impossible to get the guns out without horses, as lorries could not move over the shell-pocked ground. He sent a runner back with the reply that with the Colonel's permission, he did not propose to move till the morning. The Colonel's answer, which arrived with a team of horses that the Adjutant had borrowed from a heavy battery, was a masterpiece of terse but vivid prose.

The story of the following days is best told by the Adjutant.

The battle re-opened at daybreak. By five o'clock I was in communication with all our batteries. The 9.2 ins. were crawling back towards the Somme, and the 6 in. howitzers firing merrily away in front of Fremicourt. Throughout the day the enemy advanced slowly but surely. Vaulx fell, and in the afternoon we heard that the infantry were fighting round our old headquarters in Beugny. Major Carter, observing from a crest a few hundred yards in front of his battery, engaged the Germans pouring out of Vaulx at a range of about a thousand yards. I met him soon afterwards riding back to look for a new position. White with excitement and lack of sleep, he told me he had seen his shells cutting great lanes in the enemy ranks as a scythe mows down the grass. I stood on a high bank which commanded a fine view up the Cambrai road as far as Fremicourt. The light was just beginning to fail. All round me batteries were in action; even the distant fields sparkled with countless tiny flashes. A heavy barrage was bursting on the far ridge. Along the road a slow stream of traffic was moving towards Bapaume, first waves of the tide that rolled westward for days and days. Here and there a battery in retreat, walking wounded in twos and threes, an odd lorry or two, a staff car, bearing with undignified speed the dignified sign of Corps Headquarters, a column of horse transport and a batch of German prisoners. It was with something approaching a shock that I realised everything was moving the wrong way. Rumour was busy. It was said that the German cavalry were actually in sight, and men turned their heads and stared curiously into the distance, but there was no sign of panic.

That evening orders were received to move our batteries west of Bapaume. The Colonel decided to establish his headquarters in Grevillers, where the Corps Heavy Artillery H. Q. were still living in a suite of well-furnished Nissen huts on top of a hill. Whilst the Colonel went off to reconnoitre for battery positions, I climbed up the broad duck-board path which led to the stately homes of the staff. The lawn was as neat as ever, the garden, fringed with its decorous row of huts, had never looked better. In the middle of the lawn stood the trophy, a German field gun, resplendent in a new coat of paint. Sleek, gentlemanly clerks, carrying papers, hurried in and out of the offices. I reported to the Staff Captain, and asked about rations and ammunition. I then turned into the Counter-Battery Office, where one could always rely on hearing the latest news.

"Any one in?" I asked a clerk, who was quietly packing up a typewriter.

"Oh, no, sir," in a surprised tone, "they are all in the mess having dinner." I went into the mess.

"Come in, Butler. Have some dinner," said the Counter-Battery Colonel affably.

"I haven't got time."

"Have a drink then. Excuse the candles. The electric light plant is being packed up."

So I passed a pleasant ten minutes hearing how we had attacked up north and captured Lens and Ostend, how the big mines in the Cambrai road had not been blown as the keys were kept in Demicourt, and by the time the sappers sent over for them, Demicourt had been surrounded and captured; how the Fifth Army on our right was in full retreat, but the Americans were arriving in thousands; how the nth Brigade had lost more than half its guns, and how poor A, and young B and old C, and many more besides had been killed. We discussed the unaccountable silence of the enemy artillery on the night of the 21st, and why, even granted that they were engaged in moving forward their guns, they had not made use of their long range railway pieces. Two or three of these dropping their big shells on the Bapaume- Cambrai road would have made all the difference. As it was, everything had been able to get away undisturbed.

* * * * * *

"Wake up! Wake up"! I stirred drowsily. The Colonel shook me. "Wake up," he said abruptly. Still half asleep, I sat up rubbing my eyes. It was quite dark. The atmosphere of the little hut was thick. "Read this!" The Colonel thrust a message form into my hand and switched on his lamp.

The enemy has broken through at Mory. We have no troops left to put into the line, VI Corps.

Outside, but far away, I could hear the galloping rumble of heavy gun fire. The Colonel was lacing up his boots.

"Tell an officer of each battery to stand by the 'phone. I am going up to Corps Heavies to see what they are going to do."

This seemed really to be the end, and a feeling of utter despair seized me. I stood by the doorway watching and listening; away to the north-east the sky was flickering incessantly. How the guns were pounding away! Suddenly a great flash lit up the night. *Bang! Bang! Bang! Bang!* a 60-pounder battery at the end of the village had opened fire. The shells tore through the cold night air with a blasting roar, and the ruins echoed and re-echoed. A howitzer battery just in front began firing. What were they shooting at? What was happening? Then I saw the light of the Colonel's lamp coming back down the duck-board path.

"False alarm, Butler," he cried scornfully. "It's only an S O S from Mory. The Guards Division is in the line there. The man who sent that message ought to be shot. Give me the telephone." He took up the receiver. "Colonel Carp speaking. Is that you, Merredew? Take down this target. Fire twenty rounds into Mory, M-o-r-y, Damn it, M-O-R-Y, Mory. Get them off as quick as you can. Yes, anywhere in Mory. Come on exchange, get me another battery."

After breakfast the Colonel went off in the car round the batteries, and I spent the morning endeavouring to obtain rations, ammunition, and lorries. Lorries, lorries, lorries! The cry was always for more lorries. Batteries could not move or fight without them. One lorry held only fifty rounds of 6 in. howitzer ammunition, but I saw twenty of these precious vehicles loaded with the electric lighting set, kitchen range, arm-chairs, and other furniture of the Corps H. A. who were moving their headquarters with all speed. As soon as they had gone I moved gratefully into their evacuated huts, and was preparing to enjoy the unusual comfort of my surroundings when I heard a sound that to my dying day I shall never forget. Bagpipes! I heard the trumpets of the French cavalry screaming their wonderful song of triumph after the Armistice, but never music that so stirred the soul as that of the sobbing, skirling pipes of the 51st Division playing their survivors back to the battle. I stood outside and watched those grim Highlanders swing past; every man in step, every man bronzed, resolute, unafraid. Could these be the weary, dirty men who were limping past us yesterday in twos and threes, asking pitifully how much further to Achiet-le-Grand? I shivered with pride. It was magnificent.

At mid-day Wally, of the A. S. C., came in, and reported that he had only fifty-five lorries available should we have to move again that night. I told him that I had heard the ration dump at Achiet-le-Grand had been evacuated, and suggested he should take a lorry there and collect as much rum as possible for distribution to the batteries, who would probably need it during the next two or three nights. He had hardly gone when the

2XX BATTERY IN ACTION NEAR BAPAUME, 23RD MARCH, 1918

Colonel and the Signals officer returned. The back of the Vauxhall was loaded with a case of champagne, two cases of whisky, and boxes of cigars and cigarettes.

"Merredew has taken over the Bapaume canteen," said the Colonel, chuckling, in answer to my look of inquiry. "2XX is in action just outside, and their quarter-master-sergeant is inside systematically looting the E. F. C. You can take the car if you like and go and collect something for yourself."

The news had spread like wildfire. As I was starting, the sergeant-major came running out of his billet.

"May I come with you, sir?"

"Jump in, sergeant-major!"

It did one's heart good to see the happy faces we met on the road. Every lorry driver had a pile of cigarette tins on the seat beside him. Every infantry soldier had his pockets bulging with them. Even the walking wounded had their arms full. Everyone was laughing.

The scene outside the great canteen was wonderful; it might have been Christmas Eve. A queue of lorries and G.S. wagons and cars stretched for hundreds of yards down the road. On the grass in front of the canteen were the howitzers of 2XX, drawn up in line twenty yards apart and firing steadily away, one round per gun per minute. The gunners were smoking cigars. Empty bottles of Bass were lying by the shell dumps. The officers were dining in an outhouse. A confused medley of shouts greeted me.

"Hullo! Here's the Adjutant! What does he want? Come in! Go away! Sit down! Have a drink!"

"What can we offer you?" asked Merredew gravely. "Limejuice, whisky, gin, beer, stout, champagne, Wincarnis, port, Benedictine or *creme de menthe*?" He took me into the big marquee. The mob inside was growing unruly, and the Q. M. S. and his assistants were unable to cope with the rush. Men were clambering over the counters: others, already across, were pulling down box-es and helping themselves.' "I've got an armed guard on the drink," said Merredew. "No one can take so much as a bottle without a signed chit from me."

Later in the day the A.P.M. of a neighbouring Divi-sion, hearing there was free whisky to be had, came in person to collect some cases from the looted canteen. He was opposed by a large gunner sentry.

"You can't come in 'ere, sir, without a pass."

"What's all this nonsense about passes? Do you know who I am, my man? I am the Provost Marshal."

"I can't help that, sir. If you was the Field Marshal 'is-self you couldn't come in 'ere without a pass signed by Captain Merredew." And the baffled Staff Officer was forced to retire and seek the Gunner Captain, who had usurped his disciplinary powers.

Late in the afternoon a large party of reinforcements arrived at Brigade Headquarters. The sergeant-major came into the office.

"Please, sir, there's no nominal roll with them. Will you keep them here to-night and post them to batteries in the morning?"

"Yes, sergeant-major, you might make out a nominal roll and—" *CRASH!* "God, what was that?"

We ducked blindly. Huge splinters burst through the hut. Outside the branches were snapping off the trees as though torn by a hurricane. For fifteen seconds an aw-ful silence reigned throughout the camp, broken only by the falling of branches and stones. Then a pitiful cho-rus of moaning and shouting broke out. The sergeant-major ran to the door.

"It's hit the hut where I put the reinforcements!" he cried.

The casualties inflicted by that one shell were fear-ful. Apart from some fifteen killed and wounded, an in-definite number were so completely blown to pieces that they were not identifiable. As the telephone lines had all gone I volunteered to fetch an ambulance from the C. C. S.. It was not a pleasant walk. A second shell tore over my head with a rush like that of an express train. It burst on the road a few hundred yards in front of me. There gaped a monstrous hole six yards across and deep in proportion. Half in it lay a headless despatch rider; the petrol from the twisted tank of his motor-cycle was sizzling on the hot cylinder. I hurried on. A third shell rushed by and landed plumb in the middle of the C. C. S.. beside the road at the bottom of the hill. It was quite the most sickening sight I have ever seen. Up rose clouds of black smoke, earth, fragments of bodies and Nissen huts. A few figures ran[1] helplessly hither and thither among the scores of loaded stretchers that lay all around. I ran down the hill. There were plenty of ambulances, but it was impossible to get hold of one without permission from the officer-in-charge. I wandered through the crowded wards in search of him. They reeked of blood and chloroform and iodine. The cries and groans of the wounded mingled with the crashes of the shells that were bursting outside. At last I got my chit. I jumped in an ambulance and shouted to the driver to drive like hell.

That night the enemy planes went humming overhead. Great bombs were dropping north, south, east and west, and the sky-line was lit with the fires of our blazing ammunition dumps. The telephone woke me from a fitful doze.

"Is that you, Butler? Major Carter speaking. You know those rum jars you told Wally to bring round to us this morning?"

"Yes, sir, I thought they might be useful when we get on the move again."

"They might have been, had they contained rum, but they don't."

"Why, sir, what do they contain?"

"Nut oil for Chinese labourers!"

Orders to continue the retreat arrived the next day, the 24th. The roads were packed with densely moving columns of vehicles and men. Ambulances, caterpillars, gun teams, and marching infantry were inextricably mingled. A few military policemen dashed up and down on horseback trying to enforce some sort of order, but nobody paid them any attention. Behind us an enormous pillar of grey smoke ascended nearly half a mile to the sky, spreading out at the top like a vast mushroom. The big ammunition dump, X Don, was on fire. The noise of its crackling sounded like the approach of doom in our ears. Fuses went up like golden rain, and once a cloud of Very lights ascended and speckled the lowering sky with thousands of beautiful-coloured stars. Flocks of birds passed over us in full flight from this strange new horror.

At Achiet-le-Grand we reported to headquarters. As I walked into the Brigade-Major's office two Lieutenant-Generals and other staff officers walked out. They all looked exceedingly grave. The Brigade-Major told me that a Corps Commanders' Conference had just taken place to decide what was to be done. On our immediate right there was a tremendous gap caused by the rout of the Fifth Army, and there was every likelihood of our being completely outflanked. Despite the seriousness of the situation I could not help appreciating its drama. I had just seen the very men upon whom depended, not only our personal safety, but possibly that of the whole British Expeditionary Force.

We were told to report to the Divisional Artillery at Bucquoy. Our progress there was a mere crawl, and it was not until late at night that we received our orders from a harassed brigadier and proceeded back on our tracks to give our batteries the news and to choose their positions. We picked up the three B. C.'s and drove madly back in the moonlight along the now empty roads. We could see the flashes of batteries on all sides of us, but whether they were British or German I neither knew nor cared. Nothing seemed to matter after the stress and strain of the last three days. I fell asleep, and was wakened by the blast of a field battery which had opened fire alongside the road and nearly blown me out of the car.

When I woke again we were on our way back to Bucquoy. The congestion outside the village, which had been bad enough in the afternoon, was now so much worse that the traffic was immovable. The Colonel jumped out of the car and walked on ahead, cursing right and left. The cause of the trouble was a heavy battery which had tried to "bank-[1] round a field battery, resulting in a complete deadlock. The drivers were asleep in their saddles. No one seemed to care how long they stayed there. Finally we reached our field, and turned in thankfully in an old tent which the excellent sergeant-major had "scrounged."

I was hardly asleep when a runner arrived with fresh orders. The retreat was to continue at dawn. As the Colonel and I alone knew where the batteries were to be found, I set off on my motor-bike to acquaint them with the new situation. The Triumph was not going well, and the clutch was out of action; time and again I bumped into horses or scraped my knuckles on the side of some wagon or lorry. In the middle of Achiet-le-Grand the engine suddenly gave up the ghost. But my luck was in. At the far end of the village I passed a shed beneath which stood half a dozen beautiful gleaming Triumphs. I crept up to them, chose the newest-looking and pushed it silently into the road. It wouldn't start. As I was vigorously kicking the self-starter a corporal wearing the blue and white badge of the Signal service, came out of a house and walked past the shed into the road. He must be a despatch-rider, possibly even the owner of the bicycle I was borrowing.

"Corporal!" I called sternly. "Will you start my bike for me—? she's a bit cold."

He came to my side, injected a squirt of petrol into the cylinder, jumped on the starter, and the engine started up with a roar.

"Thanks awfully!" I shouted, getting astride.

"That's all right, sir," he shouted back, and then, "Stop, stop," he yelled, "that's my bike!" But he was too late.

I found the officers of the batteries sleeping out in their valises, beside their guns, all except 2XX who, as usual, had made themselves comfortable in a row of huts on the eastern outskirts of Logeast Wood.

Early the next morning the Colonel went back to see that the batteries had all got safely away. Having sent off the Brigade lorries, I remained behind with my Triumph to direct any of our batteries whom the Colonel might miss. Military policemen with drawn revolvers were directing the traffic, which was now moving at a gallop. Horse transport was being sent by one road, motors by another. A smart, fresh-looking battalion of infantry had just arrived; the men were filing into the house and gardens at the eastern end of the village. Machine-gunners and riflemen were making loopholes in the walls. Evidently the Germans were not far away. Suddenly the Brigade car came tearing down the road. The Colonel, wearing his tin hat, yelled as he swept past, "They're all got away; come on!" I had not gone far when I heard behind me the crackle of musketry from Bucquoy. The enemy had arrived. A mile further on I caught up the Brigade lorries. I handed over the motorcycle to a despatch rider, climbed on the front seat of a lorry and was immediately asleep.

I woke up several times during the journey. I remember hearing someone shout "Halt! Action left!" to a field battery, which left the road just in front of us. I remember seeing a battalion of infantry bivouacking in the open. I remember seeing another cleaning out an overgrown trench, disused since 1916. I remember passing a notice board which announced: "This is Serre," and only those who have seen, can visualise the utter dreadfulness of the desolation. I remember entering Mailly-Maillet and seeing, for the first time for months, some complete houses. I remember the windmill at Colincamps and the windmill at Bertrancourt. Whenever I see a windmill to-day I think of dust and lorries and flight.

Again I fell into a doze; the journey seemed endless. It soon grew dark. The road was flanked by great trees, which loomed up and faded away in endless succession, and between them a broad white ribbon seemed to go on for ever and ever. Dust and petrol vapour filled ears and eyes and nose and mouth. Kilometre stone after kilometre stone went past; the roar of our lorry became a lullaby—

When I woke up we had halted in a field near Orville. The Colonel had lit his primus stove and was cooking our supper, soup squares and champagne.

"Butler, everyone has arrived except 2XX. You and Wally must be up at six and push off on motorbikes to see if you can find them. Send two despatch riders as well. All of you search different roads and don't get captured."

I swallowed some soup, unrolled my valise under a lorry and was instantly asleep again.

The next morning we scoured the roads for news of 2XX. I met Wally in Marieux.

"No use going this way," he shouted, "I've been nearly into Colincamps. The Boche is there. Not a sign of 2XX anywhere."

When we got back the despatch riders had returned. They reported the roads nearly empty for ten miles.

We all began to fear the worst. Just as the Colonel was starting for Doullens, young Straker drove up on his motor-bike. He was covered with dust from head to foot, and his eyes were blood-shot with want of sleep.

"Where's your battery?" cried the Colonel.

"Marching out of Pas, sir. They should be here in an hour."

Bit by bit his story unfolded. On the morning of the 25th, the guns were in action in Logeast Wood when the infantry Brigadier came along and wanted fire brought to bear on Sapignies. Two guns were at once rushed back along the road and within ten minutes were firing merrily. About mid-day the field artillery came trotting back through the wood, and a message came by runner from Major Carter that the Brigade had received orders to retire to Acheux, fifteen miles further back. A party of infantry came by saying that the Germans were coming on, but the infantry Brigadier, who rode past at the moment, said he did not think it was so. Merredew offered to remain where he was as long as he had ammunition, but the Brigadier told him that he had better get away while he could. There was a good deal of transport and some infantry hurrying down the road. Soon they had all gone and save for a distant crackle of musketry in front, there was silence. The cooks had just got a meal ready so Merredew ordered the men to fall out for dinner behind the guns. While they were eating, a platoon of utterly weary infantry came stumbling past. Their officer, in a cracked voice, shouted to them to stop, and threatened to shoot any man who did not obey. Without even raising their heads the whole platoon went on, and with a sob, the officer threw his revolver away and followed them into the wood. Five minutes later some tanks appeared, and said that the Germans were in Achiet-le-Grand, less than a mile away. They were followed by machine-gunners, who started digging furiously beside the howitzers. Merredew paced up and down smoking a canteen cigar. The men had not finished eating their dinners. At last he gave the order "Limber up." The lorries came up the road, the stores and ammunition were put inside, the guns hooked on, and they pulled slowly away. The men fell in by sections and marched down the road behind them.

They got through to Bucquoy, but all the roads to Pusieux were blocked, so he was forced to turn north towards Fonquevillers. Straker was sitting on the last lorry. In front crawled a long column of guns and lorries, infantry stragglers, horses, mules and limbers. Hearing the continuous hoot of a large car behind, he looked back to see a Rolls Royce bearing the flag of a Divisional Commander. The road was very narrow, and it was impossible for the car to get by. Presently a young A. D. C. came running up and jumped on the footboard of the lorry.

"Are you in charge here? The General wants to speak to you at once."

The Cherub went back and saluted.

"Get your guns out of the way."

"I'm afraid I can't do that, sir, without putting them in the ditch."

"Well, put your blasted guns in the ditch."

The A. D. C. looked anxiously behind him. The Cherub saluted again and went back to his lorry. Half an hour later he looked behind again. The Rolls Royce had gone.

Presently the petrol began to give out. The last tins were emptied into the F. W. D.'s. They crawled on. At nightfall they reached Pas. The village was in a panic. Corps Headquarters were frenziedly packing up. Barricades were being erected across the streets to stop the enemy armoured cars, which were said to be tearing down the Arras road at thirty miles an hour. Actually

the front line at Arras had not moved an inch. Merredew had scrounged 30 gallons of petrol and was moving
on when he and his weary gunners were ordered to line
the heights of Pas with their rifles. A precious ammunition lorry was commandeered by staff officers to carry
their personal kit.

At this point the Colonel could contain himself no
longer. "The swine!" he muttered, and jumped into his
car to go and tell Corps Heavies all about it.

Three days later the Brigade was in the line again
near Beaussart and Mailly-Maillet.

This ends the story of the retreat as seen by one Heavy
Brigade in the Third Army. On the Fifth Army front the
experiences of the artillery were even worse. Here forty
German divisions, on a forty mile front, opposed fourteen
British, the preponderance in guns being approximately
three to one. The distances covered during the retreat were
nearly four times as great. One 9.2 in. battery travelled 85
miles in nine days, came into action thirteen times, and fired
over 1,500 rounds. When one considers that it takes over six
hours to bring a 9.2 in. into action and not less than four to
get it out, that each shell weighs close on 300 lb., and has to
be manhandled from the lorries to the guns, which are not
necessarily close to the road, it will readily be understood
how great a feat this was, and how great the strain on the
physical endurance of the gunners.

In field guns 235 out of 600 were lost or destroyed; in
heavies 127 out of 592.

One story is perhaps worth repeating. On the last night
but one, a weary artillery headquarters moved into a deserted
chateau near Villers Bretonneux. They had had no sleep for
three days. The General found a bed upstairs. The Staff Captain and the A. D. C. flung themselves on the floor of the temporary office below. It was just getting light when the door
was flung open and in stalked a party of enormous Germans.
Rubbing the sleep from his eyes the Staff Captain fumbled

wildly for his revolver. No use, there were too many of them. A voice from behind said in a loud nasal twang, 'Is the General here? Me and my mate heard he'd had a bad time, so we brought along this party of Huns we took. Thought he would like to see them,' and two large and cheerful Australian privates revealed themselves!

EXTRACT FROM *THE TIMES* OF MARCH 29TH, 1918:

No troops could possibly have behaved better than the gunners, and in this I would especially say that I do not mean field gunners alone. The Royal Garrison Artillery has borne itself magnificently. The strain upon the men with the heavy guns has been stupendous, and their endurance, their resource, and their courage have been beyond all praise . . . . Two batteries of six-inch howitzers, near Morchies, completely broke up a heavy German attack. One battery, firing from the open at 1,000 yards range, and the other from cover at 1,700, got on to masses of Germans trying to advance and completely broke them up, and the attack utterly failed . . . .

CHAPTER 9

The Advance—1918

On the morning of the 4th of April a white-faced Shadbolt walked slowly up the hill from Bertrancourt into the village of Beaussart. His recollections of the last ten days were hazy. He dimly remembered lying on a stretcher in the top bunk of a hospital train, the groans of a badly wounded man below him, the swinging and the jolting of the train, the stuffy atmosphere, the smell of blood. When he came to again it was dark; he was lying on a station platform; men were rushing to and fro, lights kept flashing, the smoke of the snorting engines eddied under the vast glass roof. He shivered in the cold night air. At the end of an eternity of time he was lifted into an ambulance. He awoke to clean sheets and sunshine. A voice said, 'He's all right, nurse, only a bang on the head, concussion.' For a week he struggled to leave the hospital. What was happening to his beloved battery? Where were they? He must get back to them. Pictures of a dead Cherub, of shattered gun-pits, of Hugh, Tipple, Queenie and the remainder of his men marching back as prisoners, kept flashing through his mind. At the Base no one knew anything. The wildest rumours were current. Papers from England two days old, and six days behind with their news, brought the only reliable intelligence. At last the obstinate doctor let Shadbolt go. 'Of course, I know you're quite mad, and, in any case, the R. T. O. won't allow anyone on the train but staff and drafts from England, but you can try.' He went down to the station. A friendly military policeman informed him that the only train left for Amiens at 2 p.m. No one was allowed to travel but Staff officers. He turned into a hotel for lunch. The Base-Commandant and a number of his staff were at the next table. At five minutes to two he crept out into the passage. Hanging on the wall, amongst others, were five hats with red bands. One fitted. Hiding his own hat under his trench coat he ran down to the station. The train was just moving out. He waved a piece of official-looking paper at the astonished R.T.O. and jumped on board. 'Your kit is in the last carriage at the back, sir,' said a grinning M.P. at the window. Twenty francs changed hands.

It was pitch dark when they got to Amiens. The enemy were shelling the station, and the train stopped half a mile outside. Shadbolt humped his valise down the line. The town was silent and empty. At last he found a bed. The next morning he jumped a lorry which took him to Beauquesne. There was no news there of the Brigade, but an A.S.G. officer told him that he was in the Corps Area, and offered to drive him to Doullens. In the evening he found Corps Heavies. The Staff Captain told him the Brigade were in action near Bertrancourt, and that some supply lorries were leaving for that village at six the next morning.

He met Merredew where the railway lines run across the road on the western outskirts of Beaussart.

'Damn you, Hugh! Why do you put the guns bang in the open, near a railway station of all places?'

Hugh grinned. 'I thought the sleepers would come in handy for platforms; besides it's just as safe here as anywhere else.' A salvo of whizz-bangs emphasised his statement. Shadbolt ducked. 'Come on, Major. Let's go and have some breakfast.'

It was not until the evening that the full story of the retreat was told. Shadbolt's batman, who in private life was butler to a duke, was also in charge of the mess. Gunner Prout bore himself with the dignity and distinction befitting a duke's personal retainer. His appearance was so episcopal and his whole personality so portentous and solemn that he was always known as *Mr.* Prout in the battery. When Shadbolt offended the canons of good taste by wearing grey flannel trousers in the evenings, Mr. Prout's rebuke was a marvel of tact and delicacy. On such occasions he always referred to his Grace, and intimated that his Grace did such and such, but never this or that. His Grace was a model of gentlemanly behaviour, a pattern which gunner officers might do well to follow, but could not hope to emulate.

'What a pity we haven't got any of that loot from the canteen left, I should like to drink the Major's health in something better than this washy beer,' said Tipple.

'Yes,' went on the Cherub, 'you missed something at Bapaume, Major. You ought to have seen Tipple scoffing down a bottle of Grand Marnier for breakfast!'

'Pardon me, sir,' interrupted Mr. Prout, 'but, anticipating the speedy return of the Commanding Officer, I took the liberty of concealing a case of the Lanson '06, and two bottles of the best brandy.'

Shadbolt found himself a mile and half from his old battery position of July, 1916. The zone of fire was almost the same. Again the Germans held Serre, again he walked up to the same O. P.'s and looked out on the same trenches and strong points. How many lives had been lost during the last two years? How much blood poured out in vain?

Whilst the bulk of the heavy artillery was engaged in the serious fighting which now took place in Flanders, Colonel Carp's Brigade remained in this sector until the battles of August and September finally broke down the enemy's resistance, and all the British Armies moved forward in their last great advance. The batteries had the good fortune to be almost continuously in support of the New Zealanders, than whom there were no finer troops in the whole of the Third Army. These big, cheerful men used to wander into the mess at Beaussart for a friendly talk over a drink, and the gunner officers returned their visits to the company messes in the line.

One evening, one of their officers announced that he had located an enemy trench mortar which could be observed from a short sap leading out into No Man's Land. Shadbolt promised to come and shoot it up the next morning. He arrived at company headquarters at 7 a.m., and set off with the New Zealander to find the sap. At last the latter announced, 'This is about the spot but it has been shelled a bit since I was last here, and we shall have to crawl on our stomachs about twenty yards, to get into the sap.' They crawled. Eventually they slid down into a little trench. 'Here is the sap,' said the infantry officer, 'at least I think it is. I will just make sure.' He put his head cautiously over the top. Not ten yards away were three Germans cooking breakfast. They had crawled almost into an enemy listening-post.

A night or two later Queenie was working out tables for a concentration in the O. P. dug-out when a large Belgian hare lopped down the steps, sat up on her hind legs, took one look at him, and ran back into the trench. Soon afterwards a terrified linesman almost fell into the dug-out.

'What's the matter, Randall?' said Queenie.

'Oh, sir!' the man exclaimed, 'I have just been chased down the trench by the biggest rat I've ever seen in my life!'

Aeroplane shoots on hostile batteries took place daily. Much wire-cutting and destruction of machine gun nests were also carried out for the infantry. On one occasion the Brigadier of a neighbouring Infantry Brigade sent an infuriated memo to the Colonel complaining of the short shooting of his howitzers. General Currie-Savage had the reputation of being able to consume four subalterns before breakfast and to partake of that meal afterwards with digestion unimpaired. It was with no little trepidation therefore that the Cherub, who had been at the O. P. on the day in question, set forth to make what explanation he could. Arriving at the Great Man's dug-out he walked trembling down the steps. The General, clad only in a shirt, was sitting on the edge of his bed, shaving. He produced a fuse, which he declared had arrived from a westerly direction. The Cherub pointed out the German marking on its nose and base. The General was not accustomed to being contradicted, but it is impossible for the fiercest subaltern-eater to roar properly without his trousers. They subsequently had breakfast together and the Cherub, wearing the complacent smile of a lion-tamer, devoured eggs and bacon before the astonished staff.

A month later a battery of 18-pounders came into action near 2XX and the officers of the. two units decided to mess together in the large farm-house which Shadbolt had commandeered at the end of the village. For many weeks these two units were almost the only inhabitants, as Beaussart had attained an unenviable reputation in the neighbourhood. True, the village was shelled daily and nightly by the enemy, but always at regular hours and in definite areas. The deep-mined dug-outs constructed on the battery, and the cellars under the men's billets prevented the heavy casualties that might otherwise have occurred. Shadbolt used to wake to the sound of flocks of scurrying shells whistling over the roof of his dug-out. Through the little window at the back, the whole village seemed to be going up in reddish-grey smoke. Another summer's day had begun in 'bright, breezy, bracing, bloody Beaussart!' Five minutes later all was quiet again. Mr. Prout would announce that the Major's bath was ready, and he would step into the tin-bath on the lawn behind the house and revel in nakedness and sunshine, and the early morning song of the birds. At mid-day everyone would go to ground again for ten minutes, and again about ten o'clock at night. It was not always easy to remember the evening curfew as the mess had now got possession of a piano in addition to the gramophone. The field battery would be asking the heavies in a rousing chorus whether they knew, 'The Muffin Man who lives in Armentieres,' when the first crash outside would send the whole laughing crowd tumbling into the signallers' cellar down below.

The Colonel also did his best to add to the gaiety of nations by displaying a latent genius in the invention of code names. Everything had its code name, batteries, O. P.'s, targets, ammunition dumps; even all the correspondence was thus labelled. Instead of referring to his memo No. H/Q24672 of the 16th inst. he would simply write 're Clara.' All lists of S O S targets, hostile batteries, night firing programmes, and aeroplane shoots were labelled with the names of well-known actresses or film-stars. A telegram from Brigade which read, 'Are you engaging Gladys Cooper?' meant, 'Are you firing Night-Firing Programme No. So-and-So?' Amendments were suitably and ingeniously named. An elderly Battery Commander, rather deficient in humour, was wakened out of his first sleep one night and the following cryptic message thrust into his hand, 'Have you got Twins?' This was an amendment to 'Violet Loraine,' a night programme, which included certain well-known road junctions and communication trenches.

It was during this period, between April and August, 1918, that the German big gun known as 'Big Bertha' bombarded Paris. The gun was in action near St. Quentin, and so great was the range, approximately eighty miles, that the enemy Battery Commander had to allow for the rotation of the earth when making out his calculations before shooting. The actual size of the shell was not very large, probably about the same as the 5-9 in., and the material damage effected was negligible. The object aimed at was to lower the morale of the citizens of Paris, and, through them, that of the whole French people. With a similar end in view, the Germans had constructed a further four hundred of these guns, their intention being to line the coast near Calais should they be successful in their offensive in Flanders, and shell London.

The incalculable value of morale, both of armies and of peoples, was fully appreciated at this stage by all the belligerents. The spirit of man, under the conditions that exist in war, is affected unfavourably by a number of factors, among which may be mentioned fear, need of food, lack of sleep, weight of responsibility and the continuous endurance of shell-fire. At the other end of the scale, discipline, patriotism and a confidence

Big Bertha Shelling Paris, April, 1918

and belief in inevitable justice assisted the individual to rise superior to the infectious elements of depression and defeat. The heavy losses suffered during the retreat, the perpetual fighting against overwhelming odds, and the endless marching before a pursuing enemy, had for the time being seriously affected the morale of the British Army. But they were not a beaten army. It was astonishing to see how quickly the flagging infantry recovered after a few hours of rest and sleep. The indomitable spirit of these gallant men was never more clearly shown than in the dark days of March and early April.

Meanwhile, as the summer wore on, the failure of the enemy attacks in Flanders, in Champagne, near Montdidier and at Rheims, and their consequent enormous losses in man-power, was beginning to have an effect not only on their Generals and soldiers, but on the long-deceived German people. The balance of moral ascendancy commenced slowly to swing from east to west. Moreover the German Great General Staff, in addition to serious errors of strategy, had made the fatal mistake of underrating the recuperative powers of their opponents. On August 8th, the British Fourth Army, on a front of about fourteen miles between Albert and Villers Bretonneux, launched an attack which achieved a complete and startling success. Three divisions of cavalry and 450 tanks went through the enemy lines, the French armies on the British right joined in, and the Germans were swept completely off their feet. It is doubtful whether any offensive during the war came as so great a surprise to the enemy, who never really recovered from the overwhelming nature of the disaster. A fortnight later the Third Army widened the front of attack to the north, advanced over the whole of the country described in the last chapter, captured Bapaume, and added enormously to the difficulties and embarrassments of the enemy. On August 26th the battle was again extended to the north. The pressure brought to bear by the First Army on the Sensee and the Scarpe concluded in the successful storming of the

Drocourt-Queant line, and the enemy fell back, still stubbornly fighting, to his main line of resistance, the strongly fortified zone of defences known as the Hindenburg Line. The culminating point of this great counter-offensive was now reached, and at the end of September four simultaneous and convergent attacks were delivered by the Allies. In Flanders, the Passchendaele Ridge, the scene of such bitter fighting the year before, was crossed in one day by the Belgians and the Second British Army. In the Argonne, the French and American forces pressed the Germans steadily back in the direction of Mezieres, and on the 29th of the month the First, Third and Fourth British Armies attacked and captured the last enemy stronghold, the supposedly impregnable Hindenburg Line. The enemy had now no alternative but to withdraw his forces along the whole front, and to make such use of semi-prepared and natural positions as would enable him to carry out his retirement in good order. The obstacles of the Selle and Sambre rivers proved insufficient, however, to check the advance of our armies. Flushed with victory, and eager to transform the retirement of their enemies into a rout, our troops moved triumphantly onwards. The unexpected rapidity of their advance caused the enemy to fall back in widespread disorder and confusion, and the destruction of the whole German Army was only averted by the signing of the Armistice on November 11th. Thus ended the Battles of the Hundred Days.

In all these battles and advances the heavy and siege artillery took a prominent and important part. On September 28th the greatest amount of ammunition ever fired in one day throughout the war was expended. The actual figure inclusive of expenditure from field guns was 944,000 rounds. Even the 9.2's were firing at express speed—three rounds per gun every two minutes —till their barrels were red hot and the strain on the equipment caused Battery Commanders to moderate their rates. After the breach of the Hindenburg Line, owing to the limitations of the roads and the difficulties of ammunition supply, all of these great pieces could not immediately be moved forward. Their crews were therefore set to work to salve the captured German guns that lay scattered over the blasted battlefields, whilst volunteer parties, under enthusiastic officers, pushed forward with the infantry, with the object of locating any German batteries that might be over-run in the course of the attack, and using them against the enemy. On October 23rd near Pommereuil, a village about two miles east of Le Cateau, one of these parties discovered a battery of enemy field guns, still warm from firing at our troops. The guns were turned round, some necessary repairs were swiftly effected by the 9-2 in. artificer, and in a very short time 200 rounds of his own metal were being fired into the retreating enemy.

Meanwhile the 60-pounders and the 6 in. howitzers were pushed forward into the very forefront of the battle. On several occasions 2XX was in action less than a thousand yards from the front line. Casualties were sometimes heavy, the strain of continuous movement without rest from firing and fighting was tremendous, but, buoyed up with the hope of victory, the men worked joyfully on. After much digging of gun-pits and laying of platforms, after heaving heavy shells all night, after a long day's firing, after suffering from bursts of enemy shell-fire, they would read the laconic statement in the night's orders, 'The battery will move at dawn.' Grumbling cheerfully, the tired men heave and strain on the ropes. The guns are brought back to the road, the platforms dug up, the shells are reloaded on to the lorries, and everything made ready for another long march into the enemy's country.

On one such night Shadbolt was returning from the front where he had been observing the fire of the battery during the day's battle. Three signallers trailed wearily behind him. That day they had seen the barrage crash down on the enemy defences, and lift and move forward like a pillar of cloud before the waves of our advancing infantry. They had seen the tanks, like the chariots of old, rolling relentlessly onward,

9·2-INCH HOWITZER IN ACTION DURING THE ADVANCE
BAYENCOURT, AUGUST, 1918

their steel sides spitting out fire and death. They had seen the cavalry, troops, squadrons and regiments; field guns rattling up at the trot, their limbers swaying and bumping over the rough ground; more infantry following, marching, marching, battalion after battalion; batteries of 60-pounders, the heavy Clydesdales plodding patiently forward, the drivers nodding in their saddles, the big guns rumbling behind. Shadbolt was very tired. As he walked slowly and heavily over the shell-shattered fields he noted, half-unconsciously, an overturned limber with its team of dead horses, the twisted coils of rusty wire, a stranded tank, the grotesque attitudes of the dead as they lay in the moonlight. Suddenly he seemed to see an even mightier army than they had seen that day. Infantry, cavalry, and artillery, the armies of 1915, of the Somme, the armies of Arras, of Messines and the Salient, they moved towards him with shining faces, and the roar of their coming was like the sound of the sea when the tide is on the turn. These were the men who had died that victory might in the end be ours. 'The Army of the Dead marched forward with the Living in the last Valley of Decision.'

'Look out, sir, you was walking straight into that big crater.'

Shadbolt shook himself awake. They had passed the overturned limber; in front lay the wounded mammoth, moon-splashed, immovable, and to the left the long stream of traffic on the narrow road rolled endlessly eastward. They trudged on. Ten days before the end, the battery was in action before Le Quesnoy. Merredew had left to command a battery in the north. The guns were in a little field, sloping down to a stream on the other side of which was a large mill. The only road to the front ran over the bridge past the mill. All day long the columns of men, guns, and transport passed over this bridge, and all day long the enemy shelled it with a high-velocity gun. In the afternoon when the gunners had ceased firing they lay back on the grass and speculated which of the endless teams of horses and mules, limbers and guns would get safely across the bridge. The sappers were working hard at repairs under this steady shell-fire. A gallant party of military police and others were clearing away the dead horses and men that littered the road both sides of the stream. A gun team would come trotting down the hill towards the bridge and a hundred yards from it, break into a gallop. 'Hooray! they are safely across. Here come the next lot! *Bang!* That's got them. No, it hasn't—!' as horses and men, less one driver, emerge from the smoke, and gallop up the road into safety the other side.

At dusk the enemy ceased fire, and the mill being the only available billet, the men moved into its vast, underground store-room, whilst Shadbolt and the officers occupied an upstairs room, where there were some beds. Soon after midnight that accursed gun began again. *Whee-oo! Whoosh! Bang!* The shells sailed over the mill-house and crashed on to the road beyond. An argument began between Queenie and the Cherub as to whether a retirement to the cellar would not be sound policy. *CRASH!* and Shadbolt woke up, soaked to the skin, his bedclothes in ribbons—unhurt! The shell had come through the roof and burst in the attic above, upsetting a bucket of water and ripping a great hole in the ceiling.

At this critical moment Mr. Prout appeared, dignified and urbane even at that hour. 'Excuse me, sir, but before retiring to rest I deemed it advisable to put the officers' kits in the cellar. I have laid out your valise and placed your flannel trousers and a clean shirt under the pillow.'

The next day they moved forward again and supported the New Zealanders in the assault on Le Quesnoy. The brigade car was the first to enter the town, where the Colonel, to his intense embarrassment, was soundly kissed by a grateful old woman. He was so unnerved that on his return to headquarters he poured himself out a tumblerful of neat gin and started to drink, thinking it was water. His staff watched him with amusement. Expressions of astonishment, anger, defiance, and gratification chased each other in succession across his face as without a word, he emptied the tumbler.

Alone 2XX went forward into the Forest of Mormal. It was here, on the 8th of November, that news was received that Merredew had been killed four days earlier at Moen on the Scheldt.

Very early on the last morning Shadbolt was watching the men dragging the heavy howitzers into a little clearing in the wood. The day was grey and overcast and the raindrops from a recent shower were dripping sadly off the trees. Above them a few pigeons, disturbed by the movements and cries of the men, circled and wheeled. A despatch rider rode up and handed him a message form. 'Hostilities will cease at 11 a.m. to-day. A.A.A. No firing will take place after this hour.' He sat down on the stump of a tree. In any case, the order did not affect them. The enemy was already out of range, and they could move no further.

* * * * * *

This then, was the end. Visions of the early days, their hopes and ambitions, swam before his eyes. He saw again his pre-historic howitzer in the orchard at Festubert, and Alington's long legs moved towards him through the trees. He was back with the Australians in their dug-out below Pozieres. He saw the long slope of the hill at Heninel, covered with guns, ammunition dumps, tents and dug-outs. Ypres, the Salient, Trois Tours, St. Julien—the names made unforgettable pictures in his mind, Happy days at Beugny and Beaussart, they were gone and the bad ones with them. Hugh was gone, and Tyler and little Rawson; Sergeant Powell, that brave old man; Elliot and James and Johnson—the names of his dead gunners strung themselves before him. This was the very end. What good had it all been? To serve what purpose had they all died? For the moment he could find no answer. His brain was too numb with memories.

'Mr. Straker.'

'Sir.'

'You can fall the men out for breakfast. The war is over.

'Very good, sir.'

Overhead the pigeons circled and wheeled.

Epilogue

My story is finished and while I have been writing the spate of war books has grown into a flood, a rather turgid flood, bearing on its waters a quantity of salvage which might perhaps have been better left to the sanitary authorities.

I have fired off all my guns and howitzers. It is too late now for me to rectify any omissions in my narrative. That I have made no mention of what may be called the 'sexual' side of war is not due to any deliberate intent. I have not mentioned it because it did not come into our lives. We were always in action in the line and in consequence had neither the time nor the opportunity to indulge in amorous adventures. The terrible temptations, which apparently abounded in rest billets and base camps, were mercifully withheld from us. As for latrines, their importance has always seemed to me hygienic rather than literary.

I have only written of the war as I saw it from my own restricted viewpoint. Every story told herein is a true story put down as it actually happened and every character mentioned is drawn from life. As many of them are still alive, their names and certain clearly recognisable traits, have been altered for obvious reasons.

The big guns are rusting and mouldering in their forts and hiding places, the captains and the kings are departed, but the tumult and the shouting have not died, especially the shouting. Those who think that they are going to end war by shouting about its filth and horrors, those who shout back at them for muck-raking, those who shout that there will never be another war because the last one was so unpleasant, all seem to me to be on the wrong tack. The cessation of war can only be brought about by a change of mental and spiritual outlook on the part of the peoples. This change seems to be gradually taking place but it is too big a thing to be much affected by shouting.

With the younger generation who have not fought, rest the decisions of the future. It is their mental and spiritual outlook which is going to influence the ultimate fate of the nations. The contemplation of suffering bravely borne, of death and mutilation outfaced, of the spirit of cheerfulness and good comradeship upheld under conditions of difficulty and danger hitherto undreamed of, will not debase their minds. The qualities of courage, self-sacrifice, and uncomplaining endurance are not less praise-worthy when they shine in a setting no longer war-like. The lives of those who fought afforded us examples of these virtues and it is in the quiet and faithful recording of them that the true apologia of the war book lies. This is the last thought in my mind as I add my own to that swelling torrent, whose violence will so soon be absorbed and lost in the calm, still river of History.

Pigeon Hoo, Tenterden
May 9th, 1930